2020 VISIONS

Home

Housing Scotland 2000-2020

Edited by Neil Baxter

First published 2017 by

The Royal Incorporation of Architects in Scotland

First in a series of four *2020 Visions*:

Home (2017)*, Health and Education* (2018)

Industy and Commerce (2019)*, Culture, Leisure and Sport* (2020)

Editor

Neil Baxter Hon FRIAS Hon FRIBA

Design

Jon Jardine (mail@jonjardine.com)

Print

FlyerAlarm

ISBN 978-1-873190-77-7

A catalogue record for this book is available from the British Library.

The floor plans included in this publication are redrawn from the architects' originals for consistency- as such they are not to scale and purely indicative of one floor within each development. We have also, for consistency, opted to show domestic scale elements within larger developments which may contain many individual homes or residential units.

Contents

Williams House, Colbost, Isle of Skye

Dualchas Architects Ltd

Photograph © Andrew Lee Photographer

Ministerial Foreword

THERE CAN BE NO DOUBT that Scotland has many fabulous new houses. Collected together for the first time, the houses shown in this publication tell a remarkable story about the world-class quality of new design in Scotland over the last twenty years.

The way that we adapt our existing buildings and the way that we build our new houses and places are both opportunities to show Scotland's sense of cultural continuity as well as showing ourselves to be forward-looking in our approach. This book documents a conversation among designers, clients, developers and communities that explores the balance between respecting and responding to traditions and pursuing innovation.

Our houses are a significant component of what makes Scotland's places distinctive and they can very often reflect the values that we hold. These values can, for example, include cherishing and building upon our heritage, pursuing sustainable development, or demonstrating a sense of equality and fairness through the high standard of our social and affordable housing provision.

Scotland's new rural housing has, in particular, gone from strength to strength, illustrating a rich variety of innovative and sensitive responses to Scotland's landscapes and climate. The extent of the demand from clients for sustainable homes is greatly encouraging, supporting the architects' exploration of a resource-efficient contemporary vernacular while, at the same time, framing spectacular views for clients of our seascapes, islands and mountains. A number of our new rural houses can also be seen to demonstrate that high quality, individually-designed homes can be affordable and a positive contribution to life in rural communities...

The housing illustrated within this book mindfully addresses many important issues including affordability, access and the provision of high-quality social housing. It also addresses vital issues around placemaking such as pedestrian routes and linkages, the involvement of communities, repairing the urban fabric and respecting traditional street patterns.

Project by project, the design of our new houses contributes to the quality of Scotland's built environment as a whole, to the character of our country and how it is seen by the rest of the world. The outstanding display of Scottish creativity shown here can make us very proud.

Fiona Hyslop MSP
Cabinet Secretary for Culture, Tourism and External Affairs

The Broch, Borve, Isle of Harris
SBA Architects Ltd
Photograph © The Borve Estate

Introduction

WELCOME TO A UNIQUE gathering of superb homes from throughout Scotland. The 100 houses and housing developments which make up this volume are as good a demonstration as any of the contribution architecture can make to improving people's lives. All of these buildings, whether already built or about to be, are among the best in Scotland from the first twenty years of this century.

While it would be tempting to describe the houses in this book as the 'top 100 in Scotland' such a claim would not be truly accurate. All of these projects were submitted in response to an invitation from the Royal Incorporation of Architects in Scotland (RIAS) to its members, Scotland's Chartered Architects. A total of 237 projects were submitted and a selection panel, chaired by myself, as President of the Incorporation, selected the 100 which feature here.

My fellow judges were the London based, French architect Cecile Brisac, renowned, multi-award winning, Glasgow architect Tom Elder, long time social housing client Rob Joiner, formerly of Reidvale and Molendinar Park Housing Associations and Christine Palmer, also an architect and until recently, President of the Dundee Institute of Architects. We were joined by RIAS Secretary, Neil Baxter, who subsequently edited the book. The sheer quality of all the submissions meant that our challenge, to select only 100, was a substantial one.

An issue which emerged in our deliberations was the fact that some architectural practices would merit perhaps five or six schemes in a volume which was only about representing an empirical top 100 since the year 2000. It was agreed to try to restrict the total from practices to two. This proved too much of a challenge and

we finally agreed to make the limit three. By following this precept, the diversity of work in this volume is expanded. Those who have three projects included can consider themselves the recipient of a gold star. There is no question however that the breadth of approach and the quality represented here does represent a compendium of the very best from a remarkable period in Scottish domestic architecture.

The geographic spread of homes featured in this volume, from Galloway to Shetland, is a further indication that excellent contemporary housing design is a Scotland-wide phenomenon. Much, quite rightly, has been made of what has been described as a new 'island vernacular' which has emerged in recent years. Many new homes, some very modest in scale, some timber-clad or featuring large expanses of timber alongside brick or local stone, now sit comfortably within our rural landscapes. Unlike the white kit-houses which, presumably for reasons of cost and ease of construction, were a previous popular choice, these new houses enhance their context, drawing universal praise for their value for money, sustainability credentials, build quality (a credit to indigenous construction skills) and their subtle, understated attractiveness.

While most of the projects in this book are new individual homes, extensions or adaptations, some grand, many modest, there are also a number of larger residential projects. The re-interpretation of the traditional Scots tenement has been a preoccupation of architects for several decades. The new tenements and other larger residential projects which feature here, provide good quality housing in various urban settings, while also contributing, by dint of scale, materials and

response to context, to wider townscapes.

The notion of 'place-making' or simply put, making places better, has long been a popular topic with planners, politicians and all those concerned with the quality of life in all our towns and cities. These new tenemental contributions, whether in Glasgow, Edinburgh or Dundee, all enhance their places and improve the quality of life not just of those who live in them but for local communities and even passers-by.

In 2015, for the first time since its inauguration in 2002, the RIAS Andrew Doolan Award for the Best Building in Scotland was won by a housing project (see pages 218 to 221). In the same year, another major housing development in Glasgow (see pages 258 to 261) was among the runners-up. Housing continues to be a key focus of architects' endeavour. As this book amply demonstrates it is something Scottish architects do extremely well.

You may have bought this volume just for a nosey or perhaps with the thought of improving your own home, or even building a new one. If you want to further your aspiration, one of the architects featured in this publication, our nominations service (info@rias.org.uk) or the RIAS' online practice directory (www.rias.org.uk) will help you realise your dream.

Please enjoy the book.

Stewart Henderson PRIAS
President, The Royal Incorporation of
Architects in Scotland

Housing, Laurieston, Glasgow
Elder and Cannon
Photograph © Andrew Lee Photographer

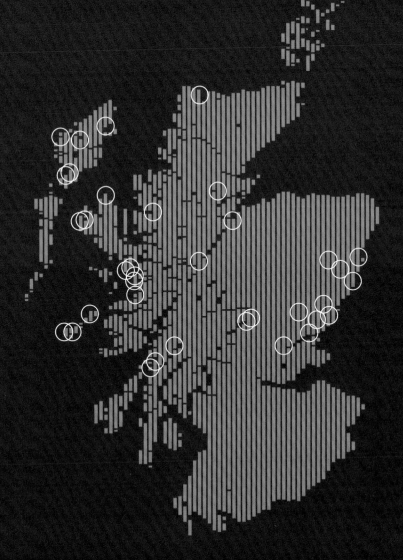

Perth and Points North

Scotland's expansive northern geography embraces extremes. Historic cityscapes, evolving townships and rural settings, amid spectacular scenery, each present different architectural challenges. The projects featured here include striated timber dwellings on Skye, crisp, contemporary West Coast villas, urbane terraces and tenements, a stone broch on Lewis and an Icelandic-inspired housing estate on Shetland. Their variety and quality is impressive.

40C Coll, Isle of Lewis

Anderson Associates Chartered Architects Ltd

OUR CLIENT REQUIRED A home on her family croft. It had to incorporate renewable energy, be sustainable and energy-conscious. The house was built on two levels, meeting all accommodation requirements and giving panoramic views to the south. Access to externally-decked areas was required, leading to a simple, grassed, terrace. Materials were to be predominantly timber, glass and stone.

The site was greenfield, on a fall, facing south. Services were close at hand and a gravity-fed sewer pump connects with mains sewerage. The context is a small crofting village where housing is conventional, timber-kit style. The client was keen to construct a dwelling that would be both contemporary and relate to traditional island construction.

The location and shape of the site dictated access arrangements. This and the south-facing aspect informed orientation. The budget, accommodation and spatial requirements produced a simple group of buildings which, in turn, reflect traditional vernacular construction. This too was reflected in the use of stone and other natural materials, largely glass and timber.

This project achieved a Category A Energy Performance Rating in energy-efficiency and environmental impact. Comhairle Nan Eilean Siar verified this as a 'first' for a residential property in the Western Isles. The project incorporates photovoltaic panels, air-sourced heat pumps, underfloor heating and high levels of insulation and was designed on low-maintenance, high-durability principles. External larch adds appropriate character to the building and will weather gracefully over time.

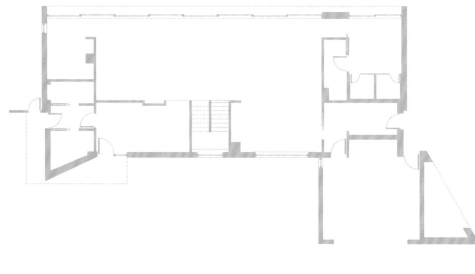

Due West, Croabh Haven
cameronwebster architects

THE HOUSE IS SET IN a cleft between rocks on the top of a cliff, with stunning views towards the Western Isles. The arrival sequence offers a suggestion of the dramatic view beyond, through the articulation of the openings made in the timber cladding. However the threshold of entry allows pause and recognition of contrasting external space – down towards the south-facing sheltered courtyard and through to the living area of the house towards the west.

Some spaces allow for a comfortable feeling of shelter and cosy intimacy whilst the larger, more open, space has a different physiological impact. The 'upside down' layout provides this with the main living area with views to the islands, whilst catching light through a clerestory window to the south. The bedrooms on the lower level have windows opening to a view of the islands to the west as well as the opportunity to look into the sheltered, south-facing courtyard space.

The materials are kept to a simple palette. Externally the random-width timber cladding to the south softens the elevation from the main approach. The roof and edges meet the rocks with zinc, applied to represent the strata of the rocks. Internally the timber linings of the stair, window and door openings are carefully controlled and considered, in response to the clients' passion for boat building.

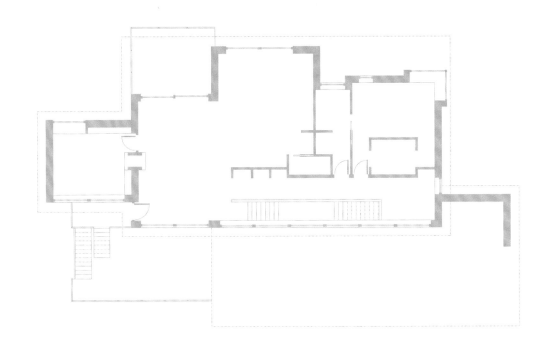

Askival, Morar, Mallaig
CASA

ASKIVAL INHABITS A DIFFICULT but stunning site. The planning application in principle required the house to be located where the land fell by five metres. The southerly outlook over a public road commands beautiful views across the sea to the islands of Rhum and Eigg, while the northern outlook is towards the Knoydart Mountains.

The house responds to this setting with two distinct architectural volumes, one volume stilted, floating over the machair to the south and one cut into the ground to the north, each with a diverging curved roof.

The two volumes meet with an internal slit locating the linear stair connecting the two sections of the house. The higher southern section of the building is where the public rooms and master bedroom are located allowing equal views to the sea as to the mountains.

The southern façade has deep overhangs, not only to provide shelter from the prevailing south-westerly winds and reduced solar gain through generous glazing in summer months, but also to provide privacy from the road.

The house has high levels of insulation and air-tightness with heat recovery, whilst a biomass system provides the energy source. The materials used are chosen for their longevity, particularly considering the marine environment. The larch will weather to silver-grey, whilst being protected by the overhanging zinc roof; both materials used in their original state, requiring little maintenance.

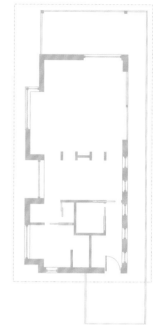

Boathouses, Lower Achianich, Kenmore

CASA

THE 'BOATHOUSES' ARE LOCATED on the south foreshore of Loch Tay in Highland Perthshire, enjoying views of Kenmore to the east and the Lawers Mountain Range to the west. The clients' brief for the project was for three new holiday cottages to extend an existing holiday-rental business. The three sites were carefully chosen to offer privacy between each to ensure occupants feel they are in a 'hideaway' by the loch shore. Each boathouse design has been tweaked to suit its individual site, maximising outlooks. Openings have been carefully considered to make best use of the location, framing particular views and accentuating the closeness to the landscape and the loch.

The houses have been designed to reflect the simplicity associated with a boathouse structure, merging sensitively within its wooded setting through use of a palette of grey colour and traditional materials. A robust steel frame supports the light larch-clad timber house and the generous, overhanging, corrugated tin roof offers protection to the occupants whilst using the decks in all weathers.

The stilted supports sit on the pebble shore and in times of high water the loch flows under the houses, giving a close link to the environment, each with a bridge to get ashore. Internally the planning arrangement is simply one large space for living and sleeping, the only enclosed spaces being a small utility and a generous bathroom with a view.

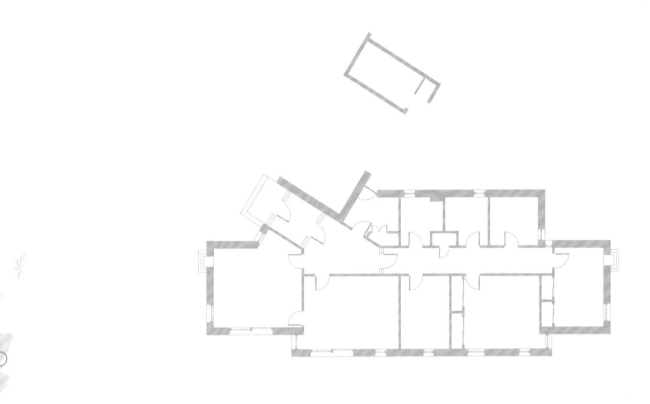

Greenburn, Arbirlot

Colin Smith + Judith Wilson : Architects

GREENBURN IS A NEW, LONG, low, single-storey house built on the glebe ground to the east of a Georgian manse. The form was driven by a requirement to minimise impact on the manse's dominant setting, views and privacy. Individual public rooms resulted in all public rooms and main bedrooms facing south, with open views towards the Firth of Tay.

The key challenge of the site was its shape, a six-sided polygon, sitting high above a south-eastern bank of the Elliot Water. The rectilinear house is positioned in a triangular area to the southern edge, with the service rooms facing north. The geometrical principal entrance, car-port and garden outbuilding are angled to complete the triangle and emphasise the entrance when approaching down the drive.

Designed and built to passive house standards, the house has high levels of wood-fibre insulation, an air-tight envelope, predominantly south-facing windows, triple glazing and is detailed with no cold bridges.

The house is heated from towel radiators in the bathrooms. The use of stone, larch cladding, aluminium-clad windows and zinc roofing eliminates external maintenance.

The south elevation is stepped to achieve scale and admit east and west light. A curved zinc roof keeps the overall form low, whilst giving height to the entrance and circulation. Use of local stone and untreated larch cladding reflect the rural location.

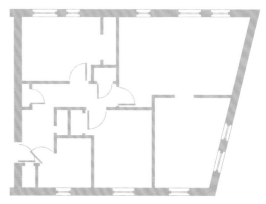

Housing, Derby Street, Dundee

Collective Architecture

THE VACANT SITE IN DUNDEE for which 163 new homes are proposed previously held two multi-storey blocks, Butterburn and Bucklemaker Courts, which were demolished in 2012. The opportunity has arisen to reinstate the historic street patterns, tying-in to the existing urban fabric with a mixed development of family-sized houses, apartments, wheelchair-accessible homes and supported housing.

At the heart of the development is a new pedestrian thoroughfare, linking the busy main street to residential areas. This is located where Russell Street, cobbled with tenements and cottages either side, once existed. This was lost in the 1970s when the area was cleared. Many residents can still remember the area and consultations helped to build a picture of what the neighbourhood once looked like.

The new buildings along the main frontage adopt a varied roof-line. This mimics the variation in the buildings opposite, with tenements alongside cottages. The buildings rise in height to create strong corners with elevated views.

Buildings to the rear, along Derby Street, are smaller in scale, reflecting semi-detached homes opposite, arranged around tree lined, green crescents. This provides a much quieter, pedestrian-friendly route linking the nearby church and school to the wider neighbourhood.

The first phase, to the northern part of the development, is due to commence in the summer of 2017. The second phase, to the south, will commence a year later.

House No. 7, Tiree
Denizen Works

DENIZEN WORKS WAS COMMISSIONED in October 2010 to produce a design for a new house on the Isle of Tiree on the west coast of Scotland. The site, containing a ruined, B-listed black-house, is accessed via a grass track and enjoys fantastic views of Duin bay.

The proposal was conceived as three different units: the 'Living-house', 'Guest-house' and 'Utility'. Each of these takes on a distinct form, in a language developed through an examination of the local vernacular's soft roof profiles and cladding materials. These masses are arranged to provide shelter from the exposed climate of the island.

The 'Living-house' is curved and clad in corrugated sheets. Containing the living and dining areas, it functions as the social heart of the home. The 'Guest-house', with its deep-set stone walls, monochrome palette and black tarred roof, contains the guest bedrooms and a quiet snug. The 'Utility' is the functional heart of the building and contains laundry facilities, a studio for play and a wet room in which to clean off beach sand and fish scales.

This third element, with the feel of a covered outdoor space, seamlessly links the other elements of the house, allowing family and guests to interact as they choose. The interior of the house offers a counterpoint to the robust architecture of the exterior, filled with natural light and internal linings inspired by a local vernacular palette.

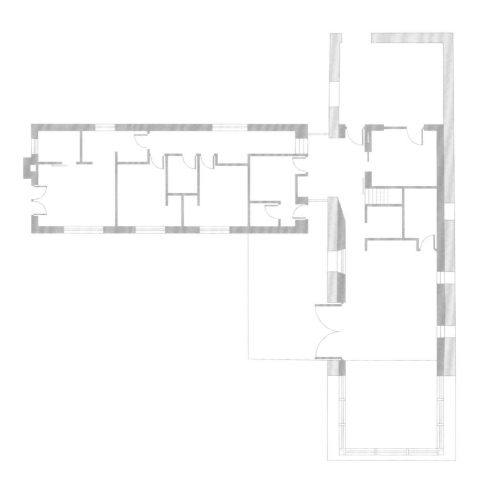

Mannal House, Tiree

Denizen Works

MANNAL HOUSE IS A NEW four-bedroom family home on the western tip of Tiree. The site currently houses a number of ruins. The existing boat shed has provided the anchor for the design proposals. The house can be conceived as two wings, one for living and one for sleeping accommodation. These are arranged perpendicularly to provide outdoor spaces sheltered from the harsh island climate.

The living accommodation and master-suite are inserted into a byre building sitting within the wall of the existing ruins

of the boat shed, which is to be re-built. It features a black-tarred roof, inspired by the form of the existing boat-shed, with the double-height living room internally clad in timber and offering panoramic views of the coastline. The master suite on the second floor looks out of a large, south-facing, window with spectacular views to Hynish.

The bedroom wing faces east, following the development pattern of Mannal where the majority of buildings face the sea, offering views of the coast. This element of the design will be characterised by white

rough-cast render and corrugated sheet roofing.

The building seeks to make the most of locally-sourced materials and local builders, using sustainable timber and passive techniques to maintain thermal comfort. Black tarred roofing, corrugated sheeting and rough-cast render all tie the house to the tones and textures of the local vernacular. The house is due to be completed in August 2018.

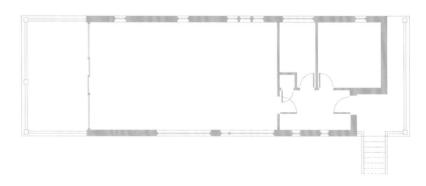

House and Studio, Loch Eriboll, Sutherland
Professor Gokay Deveci FRIAS RIBA, Chartered Architect

THE ARCHITECT ÁLVARO SIZA commented, "Identity comes from relationship, from what is around. I don't see any conflict between the tradition and innovation. Tradition comes from successive innovations".

Lotte Glob is a Danish ceramic artist whose practice is closely identified with the wilderness landscape in north-west Scotland. Her house and studio propose new planning strategies, typologies, site response and building construction detailing for rural architecture.

This dwelling comprises a large, multi-purpose, double-height living space oriented towards to the south. The construction is a laminated timber post and beam structure, sitting lightly on the earth, with a linear plan and a curved roof, clad with patinated copper.

The studio comprises double-height internal working and exhibition spaces with a large, partially-covered, paved terrace oriented towards to the south. The external construction is reclaimed stone, roofed with rust-coloured corrugated iron and finished internally with pine boarding. Stone wing walls at west and east create a frame for an evolving sculpture garden, sited between the studio and Loch Eriboll.

The different structures embedded themselves within the contours of the landscape, reflecting the local vernacular architecture in Sutherland, such as traditional croft buildings and agricultural sheds, which settle into the landscape with harmony. In ten years, through her creativity and determination, Lotte Globb has transformed an area of barren windblown rocks into a landmark where people can visit and be inspired both by the monumental nature of the landscape and by Lotte's own sculptural artworks created in response to it.

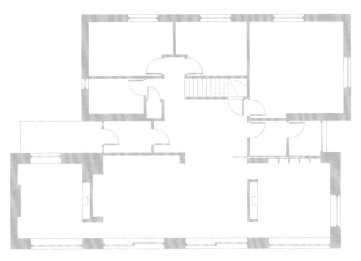

Williams House, Colbost, Isle of Skye
Dualchas Architects Ltd

THE SITE IS ON AN elevated bare croft with views over Dunvegan bay to the Waternish peninsula. The inspiration for the design was a black agricultural shed on the adjacent croft, simple in form and clearly rooted to its landscape. The challenge was to reduce the visual imposition of the new building.

The building is split into two forms. A one-and-a-half storey element contains all the bedrooms, set behind the main living space in front. It was also decided to push the building back close to the escarpment to the rear so it sits in the shadow of the cliff and recedes back into the landscape.

A garage and a shed are grouped tightly with the main building to form a courtyard. This allows the structures to be read as a cluster of black farm buildings.

The front structure of the building is characterised by a large, open-plan, living area open to the apex, giving a generous volume. This space can be divided off from the back bedrooms by means of a sliding oak screen. Glass which wraps around the gable makes the most of the panoramic views.

High insulation levels as well as good-quality windows, mean little heating is required. The roofs are constructed with aluminium roof sheeting. The Siberian larch rainscreen cladding to the walls has been stained black. Flush-detailing lends the overall composition the effect of a grouping of distinct and simple forms.

Tigh Port na Long, Aird of Sleat, Isle of Skye
Dualchas Architects Ltd

THE SITE IS AT THE END of the road at Aird of Sleat with shore access and extraordinary views back to Knoydart, Morar, Ardnamurchan and down the coast to the island of Eigg. There are views on three sides and it was decided to tuck the bedrooms behind the main living spaces to create a terrace from the kitchen for morning light, a terrace from the dining space for the afternoon light and a terrace off the main bedroom for the evening light.

The design developed into two distinct forms with a stepped foundation to give additional height to the main living space and to allow views across the dining space from the kitchen to Eigg beyond. This step in the foundation corresponded precisely to the slope in the landscape. The link between the two forms houses utility shower rooms.

The proportions, massing and siting of this house are derived from traditional forms; narrow in span and tight to the ground. It is clad in a skin of narrow larch, cladding walls and roof. It fits in to the township settlement pattern and sits quietly in its place on the edge of its world. Despite its obvious abstraction from the local vernacular it remains a house rooted in its place and a direct response to both site and brief.

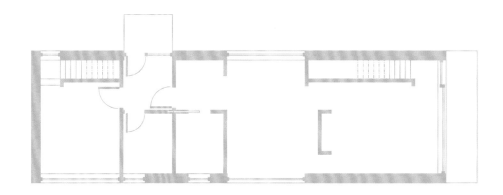

An Cala, Armadale, Isle of Skye
Dualchas Architects Ltd

THIS TWO-STOREY HOUSE IS cut into a rocky escarpment near Armadale in South Skye, overlooking the Sound of Sleat. It was deliberately located as close to the shore as practicable to make the most of the site's proximity to the sea and the stunning views. The house functions as both a private home and a guest house.

The shared entrance lobby is at the upper floor, to the right a guest lounge. A staircase leads down to two en-suite guest bedrooms. To the left is the homeowner's accommodation, with a large open plan kitchen and living area on the upper floor and a master bedroom with bathroom below.

The building envelope is wrapped in black rubber. This is overclad in larch fins which act as both a screen to give privacy and a means of simplifying the fenestration. The timber is taken over the roof and extended out over an east-facing balcony. As the larch weathers the building will fade back into the backdrop of the wooded shoreline.

Much of the design is about generating surprise. The entrance front screens the view on approach – so when entering, the wall of glass over the water is all the more dramatic. The full-height patio doors to the bedrooms give an impression of floating above the water when the tide is in – the sound of the sea and the sense of being close to nature is a constant.

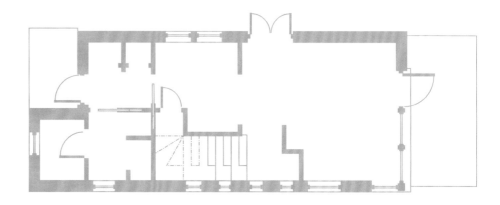

House, Valtos, Uig, Isle of Lewis
edge Architecture & Design

THIS FORMER CROFT SITE is long and narrow, sloping down to the north-east with spectacular views of both the local beach and across to Pabay Mor. The new house, walled entrance garden and garage straddle an area previously occupied by the south-eastern section of an old rubble wall enclosure. These, in combination with the retained north-western area of the old rubble wall, maintain an enclosed area that will be gradually grown into the garden on this windswept site.

A new dry-stone wall construction wraps around the base of the timber-framed and Scottish larch-clad house. This roots it to the land just above that point where the slope falls away much more steeply. The house is compact, with just two bedrooms and a total floor area of eighty-four square metres. Yet it is generous in feel.

The design addresses the practicality of life on the Atlantic face of the Isle of Lewis. Gables are set in the face of the prevailing wind. Thick sheep's wool insulates walls, roof and floors. The home is robustly designed to slough off the day to day rural challenges of wellington boots and a wet dog while offering a warm and welcoming environment. At the same time the house is light-filled, spacious and inspired by its stunning setting.

Garth Wood House, Aberfeldy

FearnMacpherson Chartered Architects

THIS PAVILION-STYLE HOUSE is located on the boundary of forest and steep embankment, overlooking the confluence of the Rivers Lyon and Tay, in Highland Perthshire. It has been designed with the living quarters to the upper storey and a large covered balcony to two sides, sitting above service accommodation at the ground floor, to maximise the site's outstanding 1,000ft views. The central core is a library, to house the clients' 10,000 books, with wide stair leading to the upper floors, from the entrance level.

The frame structure is covered in blackened timber, designed to set the house in the context of the larch and spruce forest behind. On approach, the entrance way is highlighted to lead through from the undergrowth of the forest and out from the canopy of trees. The full-height windows reach out over the surrounding dramatic scenery. The result is a robust, ergonomic and sustainable design with influences from the Nordic architecture of the clients' heritage. It is realised with a mixture of larch, hazel screens and wood from their own forest. Heating is via a ground-source heat pump and underfloor heating.

The interior is constructed around simple shapes. Clerestory windows flood the rooms with light. The wide, open-tread staircase allows for the central library core to house double-height, floor-to-ceiling, shelving. This space in turn connects the kitchen, master bedroom and other living spaces and takes in the multiple views.

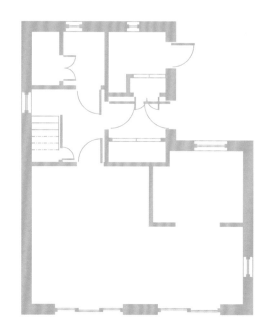

Grödians, Lerwick, Shetland

Richard Gibson Architects Ltd

GRÖDIANS IS A NEW SOCIAL housing development in the outskirts of Lerwick. It was commissioned by Shetland's Hjaltland Housing Association and comprises of 34 units made up of one, three and four bedroom dwellings. Detached, flatted and semi-detached designs provide a visual mix, with a higher quantity of detached houses as a client preference for this project.

Located in a green-field site on the edge of Lerwick's housing area, Grödians was designed referencing the 'Homezone' concept, placing the emphasis on making the car a visitor within the pedestrian realm. The design comprises of communal parking off a shared-surface loop road. The loop road bends and kinks around raised planters which act as obstacles to keep car speeds very low.

Extensive planting and landscaping has been designed to bring shelter and reduce wind chilling of the houses during the harsh conditions frequently experienced in Shetland. The planting also serves to soften and blur the lines within the scheme. Houses were positioned closely to create shelter.

The dwellings are designed to include key features such as kitchens overlooking entrances and children's play spaces, built-in external stores, flexible open-plan layouts and large windows for good day-lighting. District heating provides hot water and there is underfloor heating in conjunction with mechanical heat-recovery units in every house.

Shetland's prolonged winter, with its minimal daylight hours, inspired Grödians' vibrant colours. The layout and variety is intended to provide a vibrant, uplifting appearance both from within the scheme and viewed from beyond.

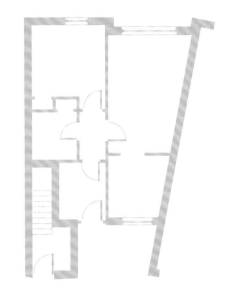

Da Vadill, Lerwick, Shetland
Richard Gibson Architects Ltd

DA VADILL WAS COMMISSIONED by Hjaltland Housing Association for sixteen terraced flats to fit within the natural curvature of the odd-shaped site that was formerly a fish factory. The decision to use a curved terrace strengthens the street line and provides the associated energy and cost efficiencies for the client and tenants.

To address long-term flood risks from the nearby sea dock, the terrace is based on an elevated masonry platform. The platform subtly steps downward to follow the site levels and the ramped walkway follows the inner curve to provide a sense of enclosure and shelter to each entrance.

Within, each dwelling has dual aspect dining and living rooms that address the street and southerly directions with small external balconies. Conversely, the kitchens overlook the entrance and the inner walk. Ground-level tenants have the use of their own planter on the balconies which are sustained by a rainwater harvesting system from the roof. The upper dwellings are accessed from enclosed stairways to provide shelter against Shetland's sometimes formidable climate. French doors provide the upper flats with an open outlook above the lower-flat balconies.

Space heating and hot water are provided by the district heating scheme. Natural and durable materials, such as natural-slate roofing and weathered-larch cladding, provide durability and long-life performance, reducing the client's maintenance regime.

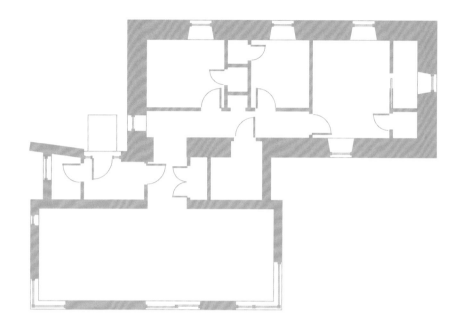

Chapel, Muckle Roe, Shetland
Richard Gibson Architects Ltd

THE SMALL ISLE OF Muckle Roe is linked to Shetland by a single-track bridge. The chapel had not been used for some years prior to being put up for sale. Our client and their children live on mainland Scotland, however, they have strong family ties to Muckle Roe. The sale of the chapel presented an opportunity for the family to enjoy having a holiday base on the isle, close to their family.

The design approach intended to keep the external integrity of the existing masonry chapel but with a new complimentary addition to make the most of the seaward views. The new part comprises a double-height kitchen/dining space with an adjoining living area. A mezzanine platform over the living area lowers the ceiling to provide a level of intimacy in the room with a handy 'snug' or store above.

Three bedrooms, toilets and storage are all neatly fitted within the original chapel. The visitor has a wonderful TARDIS-like experience when entering the house with a very spacious feel for a relatively compact floor plan. Externally, the understated timber-clad extension has a lightness and simplicity that contrasts with the existing masonry structure.

Natural-slate roofs give continuity between the two elements of the building. Detailing is kept simple, such as the subtle curve of the entrance wall as a visual guide to the way in. Since completion, the house has proved to be an extremely popular self-catering let, as well as being the family's holiday home.

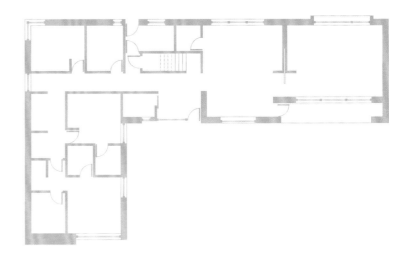

Tigh na Croit, Garve
HLM Architects

SET IN THE HAMLET OF Gorstan in the Scottish Highlands, Tigh na Croit, a fully certified PassivHaus, nestles quietly into an area of former crofting land. The brief was simply to create a quality modern and low-energy home from which the owners could continue to enjoy their love of outdoor pursuits whilst living in an environmentally-responsible, low-impact, dwelling.

The intention was that the house should look towards the form of a traditional steading, an appropriate scale and form for the site. A contemporary architectural solution was adopted, where the scale, proportion, openings, roof pitch and materials are all contextually relevant. The house demonstrates confidence, articulation and design quality to create a high-quality, low-energy design looking towards new successful precedents of rural and Highland housing.

The three-bedroom house has south-facing living areas making the most of views, with a small terrace. The bedrooms are orientated eastwards to capture morning sun. Oversized windows allow internal spaces to connect visually with the landscape and take advantage of the many wonderful views.

The dwelling is ultra low-energy, dispensing with a conventional heating system altogether. Through careful orientation, a compact simple form, high levels of air-tightness and a super-insulated building fabric the design reduces energy consumption by 80%, whilst ensuring excellent internal comfort throughout the year.

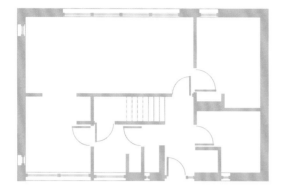

PassivHaus Terrace, Inverness

HLM Architects

AS ONE OF THE FIRST PassivHaus developments in the UK, the terrace achieved an 80% reduction in energy demand through careful orientation and a compact form, using a locally-manufactured, prefabricated, closed-panel system for wall, floor and roof elements. Along with high performance windows this provided a super-insulated, air–tight building fabric ten times better than the building regulations require.

Through careful detailing, the fabric massively reduced ventilation heat losses whilst ensuring excellent thermal comfort internally in each three bedroom house. A balanced mechanical ventilation system with heat recovery was employed, reducing heating bills but also providing cleaner, fresher indoor air. Domestic hot water was then provided from regenerative sources via an air-source heat-pump.

The building achieved an Eco-Homes rating of 'Excellent' and by far achieved the lowest heating energy demand of all the units at Scotland's Housing Expo. Through rigorous modelling and calculations based on built European passive houses, the houses were designed to cost less than £100 a year to heat.

The overarching idea of the Expo was to create a series of houses which would be a catalyst for the wider building industry and by creating an exemplar community, act as an inspiration for future housing design and development. Voted as the public's second favourite house at the Expo, it stands out from the crowd as a successful example of building highly-innovative sustainable housing in Scotland, using local materials and local expertise.

61

The Gables, Stonehaven

Hyve Architects Ltd

THIS SUBSTANTIAL, SIX-BEDROOMED, house within the Stonehaven Conservation Area was built in 1905 for the first headmaster of the local academy. The current owners felt the house was dated and didn't work well for the needs of a growing family. What started as a modest brief to remodel a kitchen in an Edwardian villa and a desire to create more light in the living spaces, became a more ambitious reimagining of the whole house and a contemporary two-storey extension.

Hyve Architects found inspiration for the design concept in the name of the house – 'The Gables'. The response to the brief is a series of gables which complement the proportions and scale of the original building and at the same time reinterpret those forms in a contemporary structure, clad in zinc. Architectural elements closely echo the existing building; gable widths, roof pitch, window proportions and configuration all take their cue from the original house.

Internally a new, double-height, family space flows into a new kitchen/dining room and links to the original living room and hall, maximising views across the garden to the south. Upstairs the library area provides views over the family room and access to a new bedroom and en-suite shower room. The original part of the house has been transformed and refurbished on all three floors to provide generous bedrooms, dressing rooms, a games room and bathrooms.

Photographs © Chris Humphreys

Fir Chlis, Isle of Harris
Icosis Architects

FIR CHLIS IS PART OF A loose cluster of detached properties, dispersed along either side of the road, forming the hamlet of Seilebost on the Isle of Harris. The house sits on a north-facing hillside with a small rocky spur between the house, the road and adjacent properties beyond.

From its elevated position the property is afforded spectacular panoramic views across the white sands towards Taransay. To take advantage of this opportunity the accommodation is inverted with bedrooms downstairs and living accommodation positioned on the upper-floor level. Picture windows and a sheltered terrace on the south-west gable take further advantage of the splendid landscape.

The house adopts a simple traditional form, taking its lead from nearby agricultural buildings. The louvred-timber screen, enclosing both covered terrace and entrance, maintains the clarity of this simple form. A Caithness stone base course to the roadside elevation roots the house to the site. Dark-stained Scottish larch cladding is used elsewhere, complemented by a dark-grey profiled metal roof. The soft landscaping of the site has been retained or restored with natural indigenous grasses.

By means of sensitive siting, simplicity of form and the use of natural materials the house sits comfortably within the landscape. Unashamedly contemporary in its design, it delivers an appropriate modern vernacular.

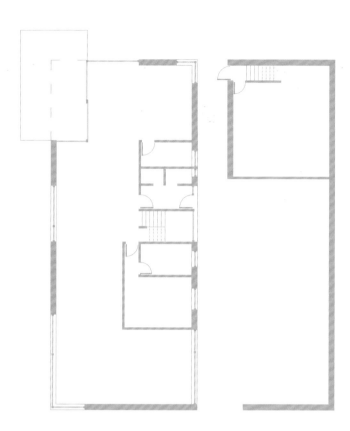

Drummond Shed, Meigle

LJR+H Chartered Architects

THIS PURPOSE-BUILT HOME, completed in 2009, is set within the Perthshire agricultural landscape. The architects' response to this setting is a home which takes its cues from local agricultural buildings. Essentially this is a contemporary and playful re-interpretation of a rural barn, configured as a contemporary dwelling. The house is linked to the adjoining garage, yet each has a separate roof form, their ridges angled in opposing directions marking this building's distinctive identity and signalling that this is a reinterpretation of traditional forms.

The materials palette, like the building's form, is a careful response to its setting. Rising from earthen brick perimeter walls the zinc roofing reflects the colour temperature of the prevailing daylight. The steel-framed structure allowed the flourish of a bold cantilever at the south-west corner extending the roofscape over the landscape and once more emphasising that this is a building which rejoices in its setting between earth and sky.

Drummond Shed's interior is simple, open and full of light. The ground floor is predominantly open plan. A full-height space over the lounge gives long views over the surrounding landscape. The upper-storey bedroom accommodation sits above the kitchen and dining areas, giving these spaces a more intimate atmosphere.

The death of one of the building's architects, David Jamieson, before the building was completed imbues this project with a particular poignancy.

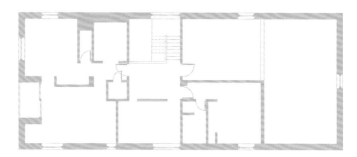

Zinc-House, Monikie

LJR+H Chartered Architects

THE AGRICULTURAL LANDSCAPE of Angus is the setting for this purpose-built home and office, completed in 2016. The site is agrarian, expansive and deceptively undulating. Remnants of greeny-grey, chlorite infused, dry-stone dykes order gridded field patterns.

Existing on the site was a collection of abandoned farm storage sheds, their aggregated form creating a large plan footprint which was formally articulated by a series of simple pitched roofs.

Buildings of this typology have a certain inevitability of form, scale, position and material expression (locally quarried stone with metal roofs) that renders them a potent presence in juxtaposition with the working landscape they support. It is the manipulation of this typology which forms the over-riding concept for Zinc-House. In this case the plan, section, form and material expression are all contextually influenced, creating a place specific response.

The house presents as a composition of aggregated internal and external spaces articulated and unified by a continuous roof. The whole is divided into four tied elements; car port, garage/office, entrance/court and house. The clients' desire to capitalise on an uninterrupted southerly aspect, whilst also having more intimate and characterful spaces, is realised through the split section of the plan, predominantly open space on the ground floor with a formed room-plan above.

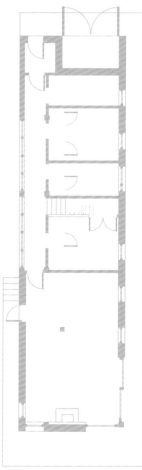

Frisealach, Glenuig
Helen Lucas Architects

THE LONG, NARROW, one-room-wide, plan for this family retreat on the west coast of Scotland is dictated by the site, between a rock outcrop and a lively burn. It stands tall above the rocks to capture the sun and view and bring west light to all the bedrooms, maximising solar-gain. Constructed from a green oak and douglas fir post and beam frame and clad in green oak boarding, the exterior wall will weather to a grey to sit discreetly in the landscape against the backdrop of the local Corbett, Rois-Bheinn.

As the house sits lightly on the ground, so too does the access to it: a place to park directly off the road and a high timber bridge across a wooded dell, through the treetops to the house. One-room-wide suits a timber truss and the site's difficult access suited off-site construction, craned on. The truss floats over the rocky ground and cantilevers out over the rocks, opening-up to the west and afternoon sun.

Bedrooms are contained within a lower storey and an upper storey nestling in the roof. A double-height living space captures the spectacular views of the islands of Eigg and Rhum and the Arisaig peninsula to the north. Cotton and hemp insulation with wood-fibre wrap provide a breathable, super-insulated interior. Wood floors and limewashed softwood timber linings are used throughout the interior to give a warm, calm atmosphere, contrasting with the often-turbulent seascape outside.

Photographs © Brendan McNeill

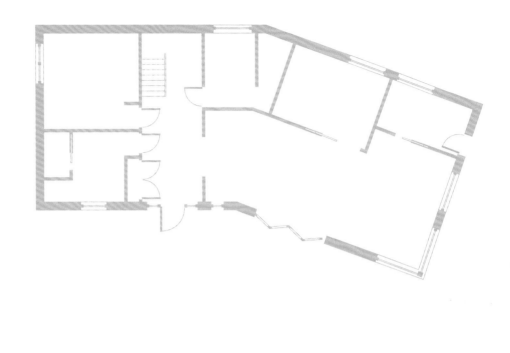

Westwood Villa, Aberdeen
MAC Architects

WESTWOOD VILLA IS A UNIQUE, bespoke design that creates a modern, respectful and elegant home that sits harmoniously and comfortably within the site. It has been formed as a result of the existing parameters of both the site and the surrounding buildings. The form responds directly to the siting and orientation of the existing adjacent buildings to avoid any impact from overlooking or detriment to the day lighting to the main living spaces and bedrooms. This has been achieved with strategically positioned windows and double height spaces on the garden elevation.

The enclosed garden has been naturally created by the form of the footprint and aims to achieve maximum natural daylight to the site. The principle is strengthened by the evolution of the roof configuration that not only provides a maximum volume of daylight but it also acts as natural solar shade, linking both elevations together.

The materials palette for the dwelling has been approached to harmonise effortlessly with the surrounding woodland setting. The refined palette of quality sustainable materials include a coated timber clad envelope with crisp detailing to create an example of a progressive modern architecture.

To reinforce the sustainable approach closed-panel timber-kit construction was employed. The home is heated by an air-source heat pump and a combination of maximising solar gains with an efficient underfloor heating system and solar panelling on the roof.

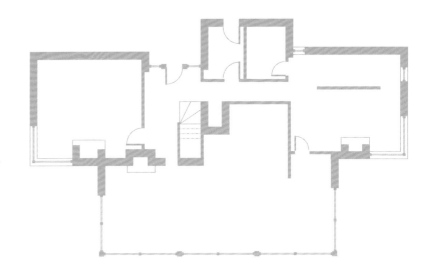

Far Field House, Kilchrenan

McInnes Gardner Architects

THE SITE AT KILCHRENAN is south-facing on an elevated slope overlooking Loch Awe and onwards to the grandeur of the Highland landscape, stretching beyond.

The house sits in a shallow valley at the top of the site which became the source for the new roof-scape, its angles reflecting the slopes on either side. The large glass box hangs beneath the soaring roofs landing on a suspended tray which becomes the external deck. The main bedroom floor sits below this, partly wrapped within the surrounding slope.

The open-plan interior of the deck level provides spaces for the kitchen, dining area and lounge. The master bedroom and 'snug' sitting room are located on the same floor, recessed to give spaces of retreat and enclosure for more private living.

The remaining three bedrooms are on the lower floor, each with en-suite and storage, for visiting family and friends. Each has similar views to the lounge above and sliding glass windows, giving access to a paved patio area terminated with a ha-ha.

Whilst the building is contemporary, the materials and colours used are intended to offer a degree of camouflage, It is of the land, minimising its impact on the landscape. It is heated by an underfloor system in conjunction with ground-source heat recovery assisted by an air-source heat recovery system which not only gives even heat throughout the house but offers a level of temperature stability and protection from overheating in the summer.

Photographs © David Barbour

81

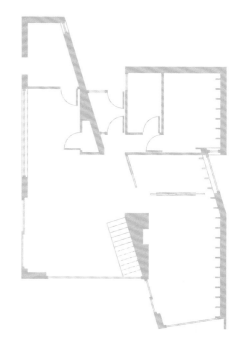

Abbotsrood, Aboyne
Moxon Architects Ltd

THE SUPERB SETTING OF this new home has conditioned how it sits within the landscape, to avoid disrupting long views and how the building itself is configured. Views out were crucial to the orientation of the plan. Located on a steep sided natural levee overlooking the River Dee, the proposal has been designed to have the minimum impact on the public domain and the amenity of neighbouring properties while maximising the experience within the house of the beautiful south facing site.

The geometry of the pitched roof has been established with a pronounced 'skew'; enabling a lofty interior along the centre line of the house but with an overall form that resolves to very low eaves at the diagonally opposed corners where the proposal abuts neighbouring properties. The centre of the house is anchored around a two-storey granite pillar situated behind large areas of south-facing glazing and containing the fireplace and hot water system. The granite mass forms a large passively- and actively-heated 'thermal battery' in the centre of the home.

The section steps down the slope of the levee to a, drystone-faced, lower level containing an en-suite bedroom and a private study. The drystone walls then continue to step down the slope, forming garden terraces to the banks of the Dee.

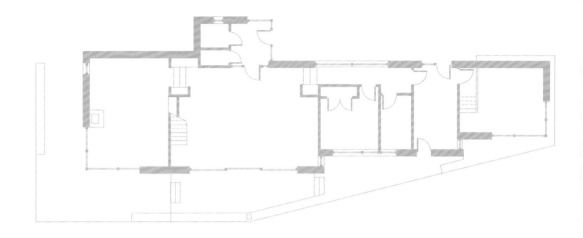

House, Strachan

Moxon Architects Ltd

THE DESIGN OF THIS family home has been conceived as a series of stepped volumes beneath a distinctive curved roof. This emphasises the way the design of the building draws on the form of the immediate and its extended landscape setting. The building nestles within the rolling hills of Lower Deeside, Aberdeenshire. The gentle form of the roof-line can be seen to reflect the shape of the distant hills to the south. The eaves of the roof match the slope of the site. Together with a, now-incorporated, granite dyke that runs through the plot, the roof form and the local material of the dyke embed the house in its surroundings.

Although the plan of the house is linear, it has been angled slightly (relative to the line of the site) to create, with the help of a garage, a courtyard entrance area. Acknowledging the extremes of weather in this rolling landscape the courtyard has been set below the line of the existing ground level, providing a sheltered space that will protect people arriving at the site from the wind and driving rain that, when the weather is inclement, rises up the valley.

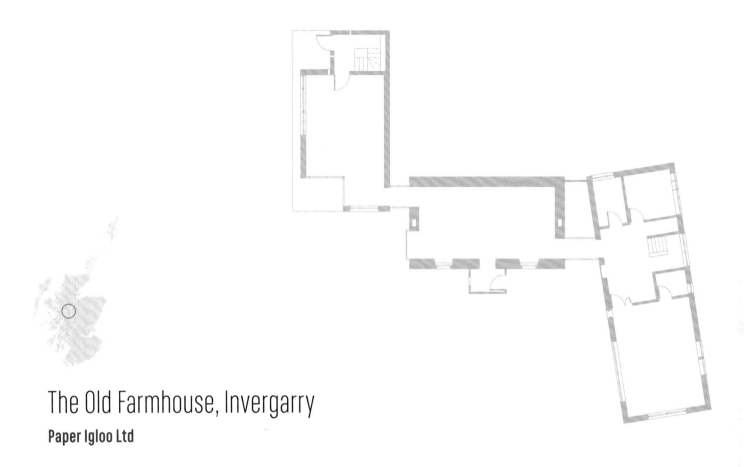

The Old Farmhouse, Invergarry

Paper Igloo Ltd

WITHIN THIS MAJESTIC RURAL landscape an existing 1868 farmhouse was converted into a dramatic, double-height space and is now flanked by two, larch-clad, 'barns'. The local built context is scattered: the alure of the site lies in the timeless panoramic mountain views to the south and west. This substantial renovation and extension of the original farmhouse has been designed to embrace this vista.

Reinstating the old farmhouse at the heart of the scheme as a lofty and dramatic double-height space, the three buildings are linked by frameless glazed 'bridges' that form corridors of light, establishing both conceptual and visual separation between old and new.

The two barns have a crisp, clipped eaves line and concealed guttering, evoking an elemental silhouette. A Cor-ten clad observatory tower, the colour of autumn bracken, abuts one of the timber barns, alluding to the previous light agriculture of the area. Unique site-specific conditions are embraced: a corner of sloping glass encompasses a 100-year-old apple tree.

The client, the architect's father, undertook the construction. Details were thoroughly considered to ensure a high quality of architecture was retained. Energy consumption was minimised in a carbon-efficient manner by both design of the fabric and energy-saving technologies.

Contemporary detailing is in synthesis with subtle references to the local vernacular; the scheme sits harmoniously in the larger rural context without becoming a pastiche of the historical. This bright and unusual family home exemplifies contemporary architecture in the rural environment.

89

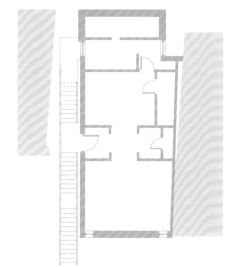

Artist Residence and Studios, Perth
Fergus Purdie Architects

THIS PROJECT COMBINES STUDIOS for an artist and an architect with workshops and living space. The building presents a tall, minimalist façade to the street with a single 'civic window' or 'cabinet' which houses a series of invited art works and installations. By adopting an unorthodox approach to plan and section the building negotiates the difficult site conditions to establish a new-build contemporary design within its urban context.

The elderly back-land workshops at the rear of the site have been renovated and updated as an integral piece of this progressive regenerative process of conservative surgery, as advocated and practiced by the great generalist and educationalist, Sir Patrick Geddes (1854 – 1932).

Initial conversations between architect and artist, long before a location had been identified, established important areas of commonality. Function held primacy over form and form over finish, there was a shared desire for visual simplicity and, perhaps most importantly, a willingness to undergo rigorous self-analysis in order to establish the real requirements, rather than conforming to commonly held stereotypes for living or working. A typology common in medieval Perth, often accessed through a close or pend, was brought into the twenty-first century.

As a self-build project the design and construction extended our collaborative working practices with artist Arthur Watson PRSA. The project also offered opportunities for students and graduates to participate in its development, being exposed to the role of architect as urbanist; not just planning and observing, but actively taking part in making.

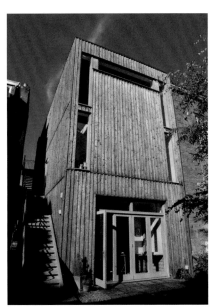

House, Camusdarach Sands, Morar
Raw Architecture Workshop

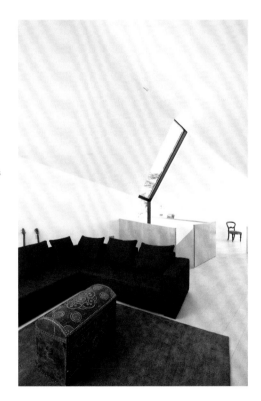

THE HOUSE AT CAMUSDARACH Sands is a new-build dwelling on steeply-sloping, former rough-grazing land overlooking the beach. The clients, a young couple already living and working in this isolated location, were keen that the proposals should capture the spectacular sunrise views over the mountains and sunset behind the islands. Given the topography, the initial response was to locate the living spaces on the upper portion of the plot, with the sleeping accommodation and entry level stacked beneath.

Construction is low-tech, consisting of an exposed concrete base sitting beneath a more expressive timber-frame superstructure. There is a clear distinction in internal arrangement of space and function across three levels, denoted by changes in light levels, scale of spaces, floor to ceiling heights and materials. Entrance is at the lower level into a darker, utilitarian concrete bunker. As you progress up through the building, via the birch ply staircase, spaces enlarge, daylight levels and ceiling heights soar and materials are characterised by a lighter finish.

Environmental considerations vary in scale and type. The building is carefully positioned and orientated. Local labour, skills and materials were employed and an air-source heat pump and super insulation incorporated.

The choice of the external colour was much debated, chosen to tune into the characteristics of the peat, gorse and stormy skies. Perhaps in a few years we might try a deep red...

Photographs © Nigel Rigden

House, Corrie, Torridon
Rural Design Architects

THE PROJECT AT CORRIE CHURCH combines old and new in a remote location on the shores of Loch Torridon. The project is based on an original church building, dating from 1887, which has been renovated to form the principal living spaces. An extension to the east reflects the form of the church, as a shadow in a dark zinc clad volume which steps downhill and connects to a semi-basement swimming pool. The pool is wrapped in a rubble stone wall and grass roof, linking it back to the landscape.

The church space allows a generous double-height for the main living area. The stonework of the façade has been 'cut' open to reveal the views, while the original narrow-slit windows have been reconstructed as a screen. A new roof uses scissor trusses designed as a memory of the original structure.

The project combines the natural materials of the landscape with the contemporary. The façade is supported on a finely-made pre-cast concrete pillar and

mirror-polished stainless-steel fins. The black zinc 'shadow' has panels of insitu cast-concrete and Caithness slab strips at the entrance and pool. The building has two staircases, each rising beside a wall clad in locally sourced wind-blown elm.

The interface between the building and landscape is a combination of the wild and man-made. In some areas the Torridonian landscape comes to the edge of the house, in others leftover concrete beams are embedded in the landscape.

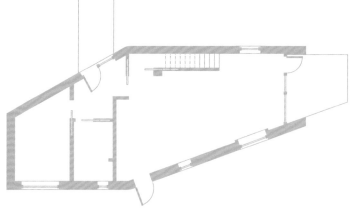

Turf House, Kilmaluag, Isle of Skye
Rural Design Architects

THE HOUSE SITS ON THE northern-most tip of the Trotternish peninsula. Trotternish is world-famous for its spectacular landforms and geology. Designed as an affordable family home for a local couple whose desire was for an environmentally-responsible house, a turf roof was to be an essential component of the build.

Tapering towards each end, the plan form expands in the middle to accommodate the kitchen, bathroom and entrance spaces. To the north, the view to the headland is framed by a large, square, glazed opening, together with a 'hood' to create additional shelter. From certain angles the building recalls the low-pitch agricultural sheds that pepper the rural landscape. In other views the building merges with the surrounding landscape and recalls the drumlin land forms found throughout this glaciated landscape.

The house comprises a primary single volume. A linear progression of space begins at the rear, with the downstairs bedroom akin to a cave. The entrance then creates a linear axis to the view and an enfilade of kitchen, dining and sitting space connects with the view. A simple stair slides up the western side of the plan and leads to an open-plan gallery space.

Simple detailing ensures that the building meets the exposed landscape without fear. The sun, rain and wind have bleached the timber silver. This weathered timber, coupled with the texture of the turf roof, help the house to sit confidently within this beautiful landscape.

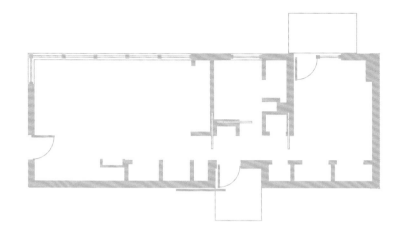

Tinhouse, Lower Milovaig, Isle of Skye
Rural Design Architects

THE HOUSE SITS ON THE north-western tip of the Isle of Skye, on a steeply-sloping site overlooking the Minch, the stretch of water separating the Inner and Outer Hebrides. Self-built by the owners, the simple form recalls both the archetypal child's image of a house and the rural sheds that sit as ghosts in the landscape, alongside the ubiquitous white rendered crofthouses. Tinhouse contains one bedroom, along with the living space, kitchen and bathroom.

The unpainted metal skin is the protective layer against ferocious storms with minimal openings cut out for the view. The horizontal slot cut into the north elevation creates a point from which to view the landscape in good weather and bad. The use of materials adopts simplicity. This approach informed the aesthetic of the interior. The recycled, timber pocket doors have simple cut-outs instead of "ironmongery", elsewhere wooden dowels are used as door handles or coat pegs and left-over cement-board frames the shower opening.

An imaginative use of colour also informed the aesthetic of the house where moments are celebrated with highlights inspired by colours found naturally outside: the yellow or pink of the wild flowers, the green of the grass, the blue of the sky and the sea and the orange of the sunsets. The external landscaping uses timber and hand-poured concrete surfaces. Together with rough, large-section timber walls these create sheltered spaces and routes from which to enjoy the view beyond.

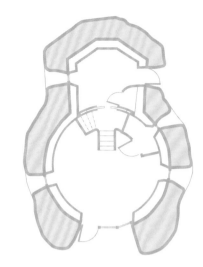

The Broch and Rock Cottage, Borve, Isle of Harris

SBA Architects Ltd

TWO ONE-BEDROOM HOUSES are set in the bleak and beautiful windblown landscape on the west coast of the Isle of Harris. The aim was to create buildings which belong in the landscape, are bio-diverse, enhance the place and importantly, improve with the action of time.

The resource and inspiration, as with the vernacular of the islands, particularly St Kilda, was to use the naturally occurring materials in the landscape – rock and heather – complemented by glass.

Rock House lies long and low, nestling and becoming part of Lewisean Gneiss terraces, predominantly rock carefully blasted from the site. Frameless windows, limited use of larch, carefully curved for fascias and chains for downpipes continues this careful approach. The building is capped with a heavy heather turf roof taken from the adjacent area so the natural habitat and flora are retained.

The Broch rises out of the trees. Six metres wide within, it is entered across a bridge to a boot room/utility at half-level. The main areas are accessed through curved pocket doors with a kitchen/diner below and living, master bedroom and bathroom above. The cottage is a luxury house with open plan kitchen/dining/living areas, separate utility and large storage spaces with large panoramic windows to exploit the views.

The stairs are wind-blown beech from Lews Castle Grounds, finished with a steel balustrade polished with beeswax. The windows are carefully located to capture and frame the views.

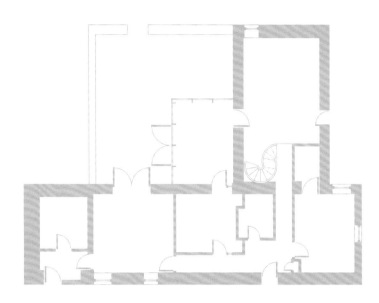

The Glebe, Farnell
Kerry Smith Architects

THIS HOME RESULTS FROM the renovation of an existing cottage and the conversion of an adjoining goat shed to provide additional living space. The cottage sits between the Grade A listed Farnell Parish Kirk and the B listed Manse. Due to the sensitive location of the cottage, the traditional features of the house were conserved and elegant modern elements were introduced where alterations were required.

Bespoke features, such as the structural glazed sunspace and roof lights and 'S'-shaped oak stairs bring to life the modest traditional features of the cottage and provide the occupants with the light and space required for contemporary living. The sun space connects the two wings of the cottage as it sits between the crux of an 'L'-shaped plan and the external courtyard. The retention of the red-sandstone wall surface on two sides of the room brings the nature of the courtyard outside into the new space. The courtyard takes advantage of the delightful view of the front of the church and the surrounding trees.

Inside, the stair forms a sculptural object within the double-height family room. The stair provides access to a mezzanine landing and hobby room, connecting the two wings at first-floor level.

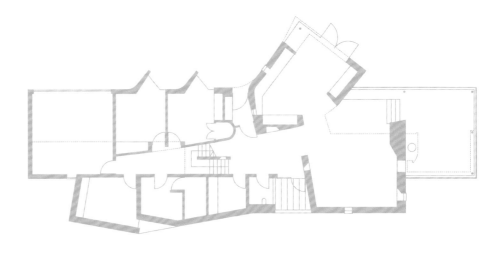

Tigh na Dobhran, Arduaine
studioKAP architects

THIS SINGLE-FAMILY DWELLING on the West Coast of Scotland, commands a fine south-west aspect across Loch Melfort to the Isle of Shuna, Croabh Haven and beyond. At its back is a wooded hillside. The site is framed by a small, tree-lined burn and the Shuna pier, cast over a tidal skerry.

The location is very beautiful but highly exposed (both elementally and psychologically) to the open sea-loch. First considerations were of buildings and landscape; how a house could be placed, formed and orientated to at least begin to protect and contain some element of the site within its influence – how 'sense of place' could be established and reinforced.

The pier offered the key starting point and a long house, similarly aligned, responds to its orientation to stake a claim on the space between. Sitting back off the pier enabled the main, long side of the house to address coast and garden, looking south-east to the morning sunshine, while only the gable braves the more direct view out to sea.

Internally at issue is the sense of exposure and shelter, how to provide the latter without anaesthetising the former. Excitement and refuge are provided for. Massively thick, creamy walls are played against cool grey windows. Through plan and section an inevitable journey towards the sea continues, passing by shady caves and through sunny volumes.

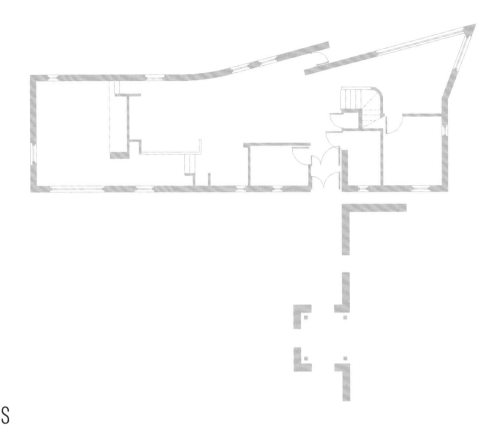

Linsiadar, Isle of Lewis
studioKAP architects

4 LINSIADAR LIES JUST across Loch Ceann Hulabhig from the stone circle of Callanish (Tursachan Chalanais) on the west coast of Lewis. The oldest presence on the croft were the remains of three agricultural buildings, long and low, stretching out like fingers to present their gables to the loch, interlinked by dry-stane dykes and dominated by the ruined shell of an eighteenth century tacksman's house.

Re-inhabiting the site in such a way as to regenerate its best characteristics, the new house is the first step in that process.

Taking the line of the first 'finger' and also physically engaging with the tacksman's house, its robust, sculptural form reaches back beyond the chequered local history of imported kits and 'white-houses' to the ancient indigenous Iron Age dwellings and their successor in the Blackhouse. Both traditions featured relatively organic forms with falling ridges, responding to tapering plans beneath. This perhaps, at a subconscious level, 'drops an anchor into the landscape'.

Though offering moments of spatial surprise the building interior is generally straightforward and unfussy. The shape and placement of windows responds to the surroundings – orientation, landscape, distance – but the building envelope is otherwise low-key. Form and massing do the work, allowing the detailing to remain simple and understated. Rough-sawn, ship-lap, boarding with a dark stain, galvanised steel gutters and good quality windows, sit below a roof of slate and lead, a black cow hunkering down in the grass.

The White House, Grishipol, Isle of Coll

WT Architecture Ltd

THE ORIGINAL HOUSE AT Grishipol (rough bay) on the Isle of Coll was built in the mid-1700s by Maclean of Coll for his Tac man, or Factor. When the clients acquired the building 150 years later some of the cracks in the roofless ruin were more than a foot wide but the basic structure remained miraculously intact. It was proposed to partially occupy the ruin and create new accommodation alongside which would be visually separate, but physically connected to the ruin.

Alongside the original building new living and bedroom spaces stretch out into the landscape with expanses of frameless glazing to capture the stunning landscape and sea views, lending a feeling of immediacy to the breaking waves and wildlife observed beyond. The new

structures shelter between the new thick dry stone enclosure walls which pick up on and extend an original lattice of stone enclosure walls around the house.

An H-shaped plan provides pockets of external shelter on the very exposed site. Internal living spaces are largely open-plan, reflecting the young family's communal way of life, with smaller areas such as the snug and study providing spaces for retreat. The new building elements are clad in black stained Scottish larch with smaller linking and anchoring sections of wall in white rendered masonry. These materials contrast with the stonework of the ruin and the mass of the new west stone wall; the black stain emphasising the recessed nature of the new walls within the old.

Border Country

The gently undulating landscapes of southern Scotland have encouraged architects to draw ingeniously upon a vernacular of modest understatement. Approaches to the predominantly rural or edge settings for this group of homes use familiar forms, pitched roofs and natural materials but often with a twist. Some of these new houses nestle into their setting while others stretch along hillsides, commanding long views.

117

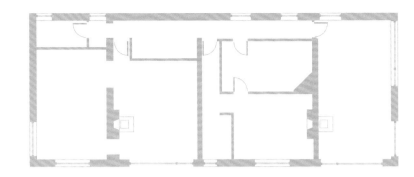

Blakeburn, Roxburghshire
A449 Architects

BLAKEBURN COTTAGE INVOLVED the complete overhaul of a nondescript mid-twentieth century dwelling to create a unique and elegant home in a fantastic rural location near Melrose. The client (a writer) works from home and the brief prioritised the quality and relationships between internal spaces. The internal arrangement was therefore conceived as a series of cellular spaces particular to activities during the day.

To the east end is the studio space, where multiple picture-windows frame different views to the morning light filtering through the woods. At the west end of the building, capturing late afternoon and evening sun is the kitchen and dining space.

All rooms are linked by a corridor (that also functions as a gallery) that runs the length of the north elevation.

Given the prominent position of the existing building any new works had to be articulated to minimise the visual impact of creating a much larger building on the site. This was achieved by referencing the simple gable form of the existing building and by utilising a restrained materials palette that was sympathetic to the context. The footprint was extended to the east and west of the existing building, with the entire building then overclad in scorched larch. The result is a refined form with an external appearance that allows the building to blend into the woods to the east of the site.

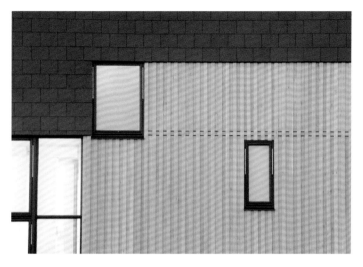
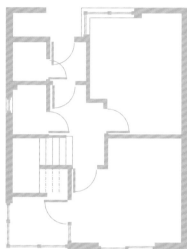

Housing, Swinton
Oliver Chapman Architects

THIS PAIR OF THREE BEDROOM semi-detached houses aims to raise the standards of sustainable design in residential developments. Renewable and passive energy conservation methods are employed, including the collection of solar energy through a 'whole house' ventilation and water-heating system, rainwater harvesting and the integration of glazed sunspaces. The construction is lightweight and quick to erect. Well-insulated, breathable, timber-frame walls are clad in cement-fibre slates and timber boarding. The appearance of a simple, archetypal form of a house has been achieved by detailing flush junctions between walls and roof pitches, recessed rainwater downpipes and discrete details conceal cavity barriers.

Rather than use external materials to identify conventional elements like wall and roof planes, they are detailed to emphasise the building as a solid form. To achieve this, the rainscreen cladding and fibre cement slates are draped over the exterior with little obvious visual articulation of the eaves and verge details.

The building's position on the corner plot of the village and its subsequent relationship with two different contexts – as an addition to a post-war social housing development and as an object visible across agricultural fields – is referenced in the simple pitched design. As an archetypical house form, responding to the building line and ridge heights of its neighbours, the building offers a contemporary continuation of the street. Seen across the fields, it reads as a silhouette on the ridge of a hill, much as agricultural buildings are seen across the landscape.

Todlaw Supported Housing, Duns
Oliver Chapman Architects

THIS DEVELOPMENT MANAGED the transition from a traditional institutional care home in a remote rural setting, to independent living with 24-hour local support close to a town centre, for a community of individuals with a variety of care requirements. A 'tartan grid' of houses mixes alternate gables and eaves along the road giving character to the street. 'Core' houses for those with greater care needs, are connected via a linear covered walkway to a communal services building while cluster houses are arranged around the periphery.

The commonly understood character of a home is created by the use of simple pitched roofs with gables at either end. Trim detailing emphasises these clean forms, while recesses provide sheltered, inviting entrances to each dwelling. Mindful of a limited budget and stringent space requirements, the project employs simple means to provide a sense of calm variety,

enhancing the domestic feel of the site.

Three different colours of stained larch alternate across the houses, cladding pairs of adjacent long and gable walls in each building, while fibre cement slates continue down from the roofs to cover the remaining walls. Efficient floor plans provide comfortable spaces for wheelchair users to move easily around their homes, with assistive technologies, including ceiling mounted hoists, integrated into the design.

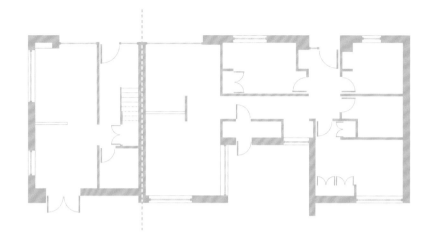

Housing, Stranraer
Collective Architecture

THE CLIENT FOR THIS SCHEME, of 19 houses for social rent, is Dumfries and Galloway Housing Partnership. Collective Architecture was commissioned after a previous proposal, for a generic crescent of semi-detached houses, stalled. The site lies on the fringe of Stranraer, an elevated and steeply sloping green field, arching around the outer edge of Nursery Avenue. It commands impressive views over the town to Loch Ryan to the north and open fields to the west and south.

The design mitigates some of the flawed urbanism of the adjacent estate. Well-considered public spaces of varying scales and character form its perimeter. Key lines

of sight are retained to the fields beyond, as is the sense of proximity and connection with the countryside.

The architectural character of the development takes precedent from the bold forms of the 1960s, the period during which the adjacent housing was constructed. Clusters of pitched roofed homes, executed in a crisp palette of brick and zinc, are arranged across the hillside, forming a visually compelling whole. This avoids the suburban character of the previous scheme whilst meeting the client's requirements for extensive individual gardens with direct access for each house and extensive parking provision.

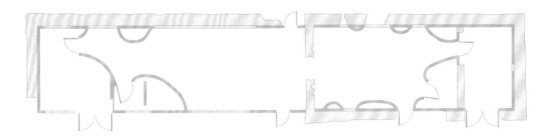

Ruins Studio, Dumfriesshire
Lily Jencks Studio with Nathanael Dorent and Savills (UK) Ltd

HAZELWOOD WAS THE DERELICT ruins of a small nineteenth-century Dumfriesshire farm, set in an elevated location just north of Dumfries. The most intact ruin on the site was a barn on an east-west axis, with the remains of a cart shed attached to its west end. The east end of the barn is two storeys, due to being set into a hillside and incorporates a small downstairs room. The structure was in an advanced state of deterioration. The design concept was to capture that state at a specific point in time and create a beautiful palimsest.

The design approach allowed the contemporary, contrasting structure to be placed within the stabilised stone walls with minimum loss of identity. The simple shape echoes the lines of the original structures and has been covered in a single, neutral, material with simple unobtrusive openings. The material was detailed so that it appears to merge effortlessly with the stone, accentuating the original built form and generating opposing textures.

The contrasting interior incorporates curvilinear and womb-like shapes. This was a technical challenge. A series of plywood ribs and polystyrene are covered in fibreglass.

Sensitive landscaping and stabilisation of the ruined remains of the adjacent farm house contribute significantly to the setting of the building. Excessive grid connection costs demanded a self-sufficient energy supply involving a photovoltaic solar array which charges a bank of batteries.

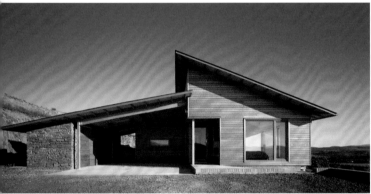

The Houl, Kendoon, Castle Douglas

Simon Winstanley Architects

THE HOUSE IS SITUATED in a natural concave of hillside sitting long and low, facing west to enjoy the spectacular view of the river Ken valley and the Rhinns of Kells hills beyond. It embodies current thinking about the design of the contemporary house – very low energy consumption (net zero-carbon in this case) using very high levels of insulation, minimising air infiltration, heating by air-source heat pump, whole-house heat recovery ventilation and on-site generation of electricity by wind turbine.

The Houl is a single storey 'long house' on a very simple plan, with all the principal rooms addressing the view and the ancillary service spaces to the rear. The slope of the roof of the main living accommodation follows the slope of the hillside with the roof of the ancillary areas meeting the main roof at a shallower angle to allow morning sunlight to penetrate the house through clerestory windows.

The entrance is sited on the north-east side of the house, under cover of the roof to provide shelter from the prevailing wind. The construction uses steel and timber frames with walls clad in naturally weathered, silver-grey, cedar with triple-glazed windows. The roof is finished with pre-weathered standing seam zinc.

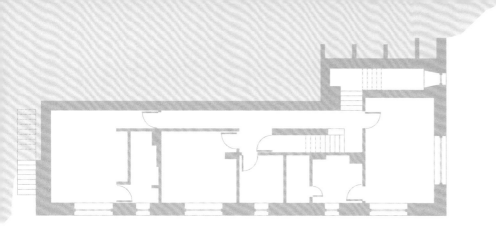

Deepstone, Portling
Simon Winstanley Architects

THE HOUSE IS LOCATED in the village of Portling on a spectacular site overlooking the Solway Firth. The site is a steeply sloping, former quarry in a National Scenic Area. The house is conceived as a stone plinth which echoes the quarry face and houses the bedrooms with a garage and entrance under at the quarry base level. The principal living accommodation is expressed as a glazed 'pavilion', sitting on the solid plinth. It is set back to form an external terrace facing the sea and to reduce the apparent mass of the house.

The glazed pavilion is constructed with a steel frame and highly-insulated timber-infill panels clad in cedar and triple-glazed windows. The roof, although thick internally to provide very-high levels of insulation, is cantilevered on all sides with projecting, expressed, douglas fir rafters to give a thin, elegant leading edge.

The roof is finished in standing seam pre-fabricated grey zinc. The masonry base is finished in stone from recycled quarry waste.

The design has numerous low-energy features. The external walls, floor and roof are insulated to a high standard and air infiltration is minimised. Triple-glazed windows achieve a whole-window energy saving. A heat pump, using a borehole, provides the ground-source for the underfloor heating and hot-water system with a wood-burning stove as back-up. Micro-generation of renewable electricity is achieved via roof-mounted photovoltaic panels. Finally, the whole house has a heat-recovery ventilation system.

Central Belt: East

Designing for the urban context often requires architects to masterplan little village communities within the wider cityscape. So the challenge with many of the projects featured here was as much about creating liveable spaces between buildings as about the form of the buildings themselves. Large tenements and urban blocks are in extreme contrast with the modest extensions and reconfigurations which draw upon the skills of their architects to radically improve the comfort and usability of tired dwellings. Irrespective of scale, the projects featured here are virtuouso performances.

Photograph top © Gordon Burniston
Photograph lower left © Dapple Photography
Photograph lower right © 7N Architects

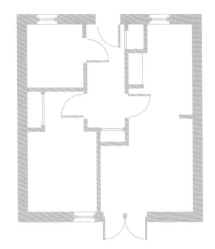

Housing, Water of Leith, Edinburgh
7N Architects

WESTFIELD AVENUE IS A development of 253 affordable homes and eight small business units on a brownfield site to the west of Edinburgh city centre. The project brings a holistic approach to the critical need for affordable, sustainable housing in central Edinburgh and has transformed vacant land by the Water of Leith into a vibrant, mixed-use, mixed-tenure neighbourhood. The buildings and public spaces fan out towards the Water of Leith, opening up views to the river from deep within the site and creating new pedestrian and cycle connections.

The project provides a mix of studio, one, two and three bed flats across four buildings, with small business spaces located throughout. Generous access decks provide spaces for meeting and socialising and enable the majority of flats to achieve a dual aspect. At ground floor, flats have access to private green space, whilst on the upper floors many have access to private balconies and roof terraces. Extensive landscaping, a mixture of planted public realm and secure private greens, is spread throughout the site.

Blue-facing brick is used at ground level with coloured acrylic render above, broken up by horizontal aluminium flashing profiles and generous glazing. The render is predominantly a muted blue-grey, with orange highlight panels completing the elevational composition. Shared cores are clad in timber with distinctive graphic panels at communal entrances. The materials provide a simple, robust aesthetic which is hard-wearing and low maintenance, yet distinctive.

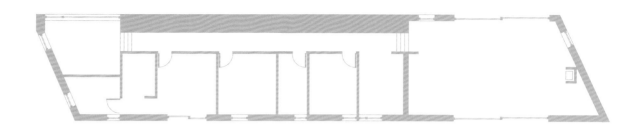

House, Musselburgh

A449 Architects

THIS CONVERSION OF AN historic steading is set in a stunning coastal location on the western edge of Musselburgh in East Lothian. Built into the robust sea wall, the existing dwelling was converted in the 1960s. Although benefiting from a south-facing walled courtyard, the original building was introverted and largely hidden from the public realm. Just one small window faced the Forth, with a wedge-shaped raised garden terrace to the east providing the only other opportunity of a sea view. The prominent addition responds more appropriately to the location.

To the south side, a large sliding glazed panel provides access to a garden terrace, while to the north another wide panel allows panoramic views to the coastline. Maintaining views to the south-facing courtyard informed the decision to locate primary circulation on the north side of the property. This long space runs the full length of the existing building, leading to incrementally more private spaces.

Externally, the wedge-shaped extension footprint enabled the creation of a distinctive interpretation of a traditional gable form. The perceived form changes as you observe the building from different viewpoints. From the road to the south and east the gable is defined and pronounced, while from the beach to the north it blends harmoniously with the rest of the building.

142

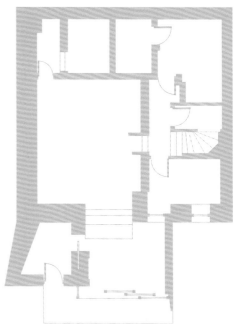

Extension and Interior, New Town, Edinburgh
Capital A Architecture Ltd

THIS EDINBURGH NEW TOWN tenement was a law firm's office until a developer subdivided it, turned the upper floors into luxury flats and sold off the two basement floors with planning permission for an extension. The basement was a store, complete with a walk-in safe and needed complete refurbishment. The new design was so extensive it required new planning, listed building consent and warrant applications.

The new design creates a more open-plan living area, split over two levels. The rear garden is steep and the new garden room works with this. By lowering the floor level to create a taller space, the room connects to the garden with as few steps as possible. The existing floor slabs were re-used in the landscape design.

The new garden room is clad in zinc with thin edge details to minimise its visual impact. The design is contemporary but also respects the historic context. The flat has five bedrooms, three of which are en-suite. There is a wine store, a utility room and a media room with home cinema. The downstairs bathroom is in the old, walk-in, safe. The existing half-spiral stair now has a modern, recessed, handrail detail.

The new interior respects the history of the flat but breathes new life into it by using high quality modern design to create a welcoming home in the heart of Edinburgh.

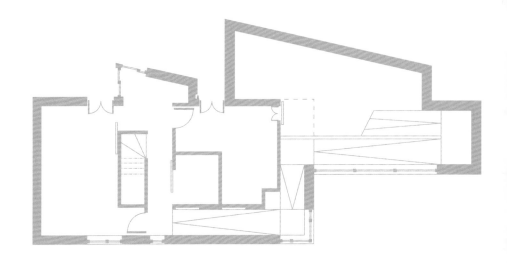

The Ramp House, Portobello, Edinburgh
Chambers McMillan Architects

THE RAMP HOUSE IS A family home designed for a little girl who is a wheelchair user, where the whole house enables her to lead a barrier-free life. The built environment often presents physical barriers. This home is a fully inclusive place; using a ramp to access all levels, providing equality of space for all.

The difference that the ramp makes is in how the spaces are experienced; connecting both horizontally and vertically, this is both linear and sectional; the ramp contributes both width and height to each of the different pausing places along the way. The design has made a difference to everyday life. For a child who cannot move around independently, the connectivity of the spaces becomes all the more important. However the open plan provides many opportunities for privacy and seclusion whilst still being part of the life of the house.

It was important that this home should be a place belonging to the children as well as their parents. To ensure this, they were included in the design process; working with models to help the children understand how spaces might feel and how they might connect.

The wider impact of an inclusive house like this, is that people who visit experience a different way of moving around a house. They come to understand that accessibility does not need to be about constrictions, but can be a delight.

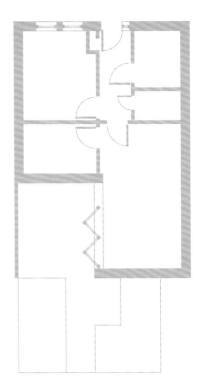

Urban Eden, Edinburgh
EMA Architecture + Design Limited

THE DESIGN CREATES SIGNATURE buildings in each corner of the site. These taller buildings range in height from six to nine storeys interconnecting with the wide cityscape, acting as signposts for the new neighbourhood.

Within the neighbourhood a series of streets, lanes and courtyards reflects the domestic scale of Edinburgh's colonies. In effect this is a traditional family neighbourhood in a contemporary manner, with people-friendly streets, squares and terraces, balconies and planters. Uniquely for such a city centre location, all of the properties benefit from their own private outdoor amenity space with balconies, terraces or gardens. Materials have been chosen very carefully, following the traditional colony houses predominantly in brick and also the sandy and grey stone hues that are so much a part of the city.

A key design aspiration associated with the regeneration of this part of the city, was to provide a pedestrian connection to the adjacent retail park and transport links into the city. Easy connections to the surrounding area and Lochend Park have been created through the new path network.

The whole neighbourhood meets excellent sustainability standards, with heating, ventilation and drainage strategies as well as waste storage, disposal and recycling. Mechanical heat-recovery ventilation systems have been installed to all properties.

One couple who have moved in commented that the development is "a new community with a real sense of place and pride."

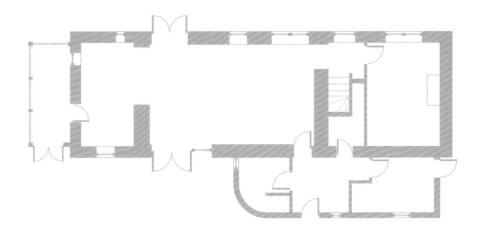

School House, Cupar

Fife Architects

THIS PROJECT SAW THE creation of a new, near off-grid, home within the shell of a former school house set in the rolling countryside just outside Cupar in Fife. Along with extending and renovating the house itself, the clients wanted to prolong the life of the building as well as upgrade it by making it as energy efficient as possible. The old, single-glazed, windows were replaced and the thermal envelope of the building improved.

At the front a new, larch-clad, extension, housing the hallway, boot room, utility and cloakroom was added, allowing for more generous living space. A larch-framed sun room was also built off the kitchen with direct access onto the garden. Losing the central staircase created a large, open-plan, living/dining space in the heart of the home with the kitchen at one end and an additional separate living room at the other end.

The first floor was also dramatically improved with new dormer windows. A spacious bathroom and store were built in the area previously taken up by the staircase. A new single bedroom/study was added alongside the two existing bedrooms.

Thermal and photovoltaic panels have been installed on the roof of the sun room which, combined with a new biomass boiler, supply all the domestic energy and hot water requirements. The property also has its own private water well, which, with the installation of a pump and filter, makes the house almost self-sufficient.

153

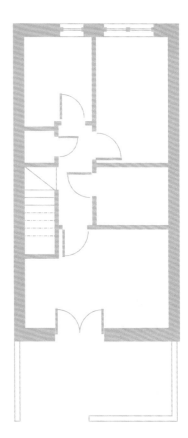

Housing, West Pilton, Edinburgh
Malcolm Fraser Architects

THIS DEVELOPMENT IS PART of the City of Edinburgh Council's ambitious 21st Century Homes project, which uses innovative borrowing to reinvigorate the social rental sector. The site was a city block which retained one tower, Northview Court, from the demolition of poor, post-War, stock. The tough, tenemental form defines and protects the whole urban block, incorporating different flatted and townhouse conditions into a simple whole. Urban elevations face north, west and south with a garden facing to the east.

The garden frontage shelters individual gardens for the townhouses and ground floor flats (which include four wheelchair-accessible properties) with a shared garden for all properties, edged and defined by bike and bin stores and the district heat plant. These gradations of personal and shared gardens then connect out to the adjacent, renewed, playpark which is shared with the tower.

Materials are tough and simple. "Breathing wall construction" is used throughout. A combined heat and power system is used with individual smart meters located in each property. Energy performance exceeds building regulations.

All this demonstrates that cutting-edge sustainability and a focus on health and well-being need not be the preserve of the top-end of the market but is attainable for all. The Council has established a cooperative approach to the property management with tenants active in the care of their own homes and gardens.

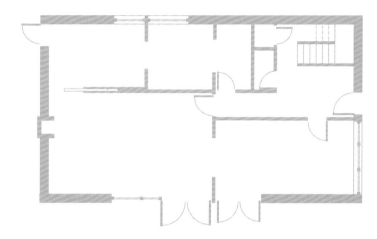

Maryfield, Bo'ness
Malcolm Fraser Architects

MARYFIELD IS A LITTLE suburban community of 28 homes on the outskirts of the town of Bo'ness. It demonstrates a new way of approaching volume housebuilding significantly different from the standard scenic scatter. Instead the rigorous form and layout benefits from careful attention to sunshine and gathering space.

Each plot is masterplanned with the house set-out to the north, or east if it would overshadow a neighbour's garden. Living spaces are then placed along the south/garden elevation of each home, spilling-out through glazed doors to a sunny garden that is now big enough (with the house pushed towards the site's boundary) to kick a football around. Paths and garage then define space for washing-lines or car repair and all link to a village green for kids to meet or community social events to be arranged.

Variety is generated from the avoidance of overshadowing and site adaptations, providing a balance between coherence and difference across the site. The homes themselves are simply and crisply detailed with investment in landscape and good quality materials, such as grey base-course brickwork, high-quality windows and white render and slate roofs. Since completion in 2004 the site has worn well, the landscape has matured and a living community has formed.

157

Princess Gate, Fairmilehead, Edinburgh
Malcolm Fraser Architects

THIS NEIGHBOURHOOD OF seventeen terraced houses is grouped around short mews, along a gentle south-facing slope, towards the southern edge of Edinburgh. A single block of six flats at the top of the site, sits alongside a wee wood of Scots Pines. All the gardens and living spaces face south, maximising sunshine and views to the Pentland Hills. The front doors and garages face north.

The living rooms in the homes have sheltered, inset balconies and are mostly on the upper floors with long views towards the hills and ground floor family rooms give onto the sunny gardens. The central stairs are top-lit and public spaces are open-plan. Mews are sheltered and neighbourly, leading out to a village green at the community's heart, a place of sunshine and gathering.

The layout contrasts with the more standard developments which neighbour it. It focusses on issues of community, landscape and open space, with children regularly playing on its green and the virtues and value of the view, none of which seem to have been considered in the neighbouring layouts. Such virtues have resulted in excellent re-sale values and a tightly-integrated community with their own residents association. Besides these undoubted assets Princess Gate is also nearly twice as dense as its neighbours, providing better use of urban land and a tighter community. As a result, there is more convenient access to services, and, where land is expensive, a consequent better return for the developers.

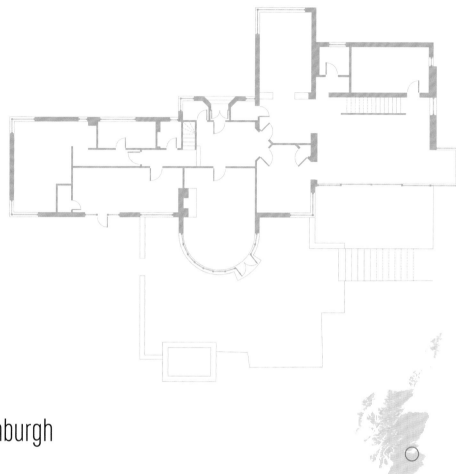

House, Murrayfield, Edinburgh
Hoskins Architects

HOSKINS ARCHITECTS WAS commissioned in 2012 to remodel a Category B-listed villa in west Edinburgh designed by Basil Spence. The house, in the International Modern style of the period, is one of Spence's earliest works from a period when he was working alongside William Kininmonth. It is located on a private road and forms part of a collection of differently-styled detached villas all built in the 1930s. The brief was to extend and alter the original, white, Crittal windowed house to suit the needs of the client and their young children.

The new accommodation is contained in a three storey block flanking the original house and a previous, 1970s, extension. Basement accommodation is dug into the sloping site and provides a plinth upon which sits a large ground floor of family accommodation and a large south-facing terrace. This is wrapped in full-height glazing with an east-facing cantilevered bay window taking advantage of the long views from this elevated site to the Firth of Forth and Fife beyond.

The upper level has been re-modelled to form children's bedroom accommodation in the existing house and a new master suite in the extension. Large, storey-height, pale concrete panels cover this more private level with punched openings to take advantage of the long views.

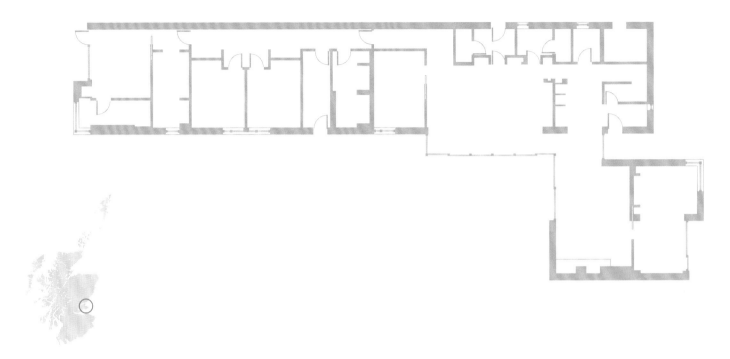

Gray House, St Andrews
Hoskins Architects

THIS FAMILY HOME ON the edge of the St Andrews conservation area sit in a unique, long, narrow, gap site. A crucial element of the brief was the clients' desire for a holistic approach to designing the garden and the house in unison to take advantage of the site's distinctive proportions. The site is enclosed by an existing mature beech hedge and surrounded by existing dwellings of varying styles and ages.

During the design process the proposal gained the support of the St. Andrews Preservation Society for its sensitive approach to designing a contemporary dwelling in an established residential area.

The house itself consists of two plain white, monolithic boxes of differing scales and two crafted timber cubes. These are arranged in relation to a straight line datum which runs the length of the site and organises both the house and garden. The gap between the two, white-rendered, boxes forms a clear and sheltered entrance and affords a controlled view through the house to the garden beyond.

The crafted timber elements, in contrast with the precise white boxes, produce a contemporary home that is integrated into the site, creating a sense of quiet privacy with minimal impact on neighbouring aspects. The building is detailed to deliver low energy consumption using high insulation and air-tightness. The continuous datum and logic of spatial arrangement extends to the garden, creating a series of carefully controlled external spaces, for relaxing, entertaining and gardening.

167

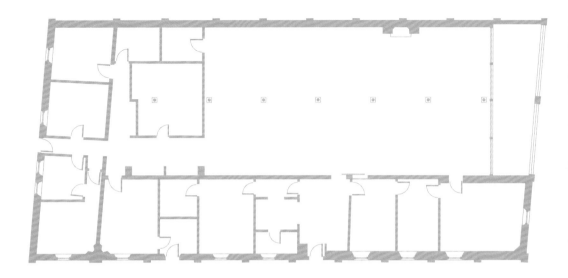

Cardy Net House, Lower Largo
Hurd Rolland

THIS AWARD-WINNING conversion of a nineteenth-century former net factory on the northern shore of the Firth of Forth re-imagined the spaces within the factory, blending sensitive restoration with the introduction of bold contemporary elements – to create a beautiful home with wonderful south-facing views.

The central idea was to create a modern living space, while retaining the unique atmosphere that existed within the Victorian factory. The original cast-iron structure was retained and carefully restored. There was also a careful restoration exercise carried out on some original panelling.

To improve the quality of the space, natural top-lighting was introduced through the roof. The smooth polished-concrete floor creates continuity in the large main space, which is enhanced by beautiful bespoke fittings. The result is an attractive, open, living space surrounded by generous bedroom and bathroom accommodation.

The external fabric of the building was cleaned and restored. The existing south-facing brick gables were replaced by large, sliding glass doors. These doors give access onto a recessed, timber-lined, terrace and provide expansive views across the Firth of Forth. Contemporary stainless steel and aluminium fittings were introduced which contrast with the Victorian brick and cast-iron fabric to revitalise this listed building as a vibrant and exciting new home.

Photographs © Torquil Kramer

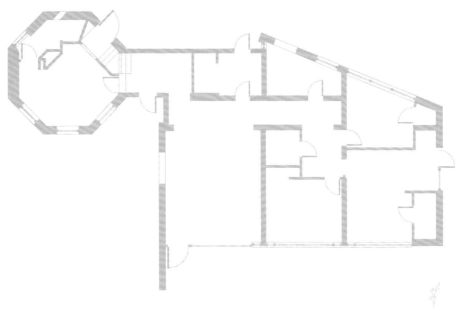

Signal Station House, North Queensferry
Icosis Architects

THE ORIGINAL B LISTED signal tower by the Forth Rail Bridge was purchased in 2001. The brief required a mixture of sensitive renovation and 'eco-modernism': to renovate the building and add a modern extension using environmentally-sustainable materials and methods, to create a contemporary family home.

The orientation and positioning of the extension responds to the exposed coastal location of the site, the movement of the sun and the views. The predominantly solid east and west walls act as book-ends, sandwiching an all-glass south elevation,

framing the garden and bridge and optimising solar gain. Rooflights above the corridor spine of the new structure allow natural light to penetrate the heart of the building

The original structure was stripped back internally to its original brick walls and concrete floors, a new stair was installed and the walls were re-lined using sheeps-wool insulation and clay boards with a clay-plaster finish. New triple-glazed timber windows were installed and the flat concrete roof was insulated above with cork and sealed using a rubber membrane.

Pre-manufactured timber cassettes filled with cellulose insulation were erected in three days on a prepared base to form the extension. The main walls are a hygroscopic construction, with untreated Scottish larch cladding, or woodwool slabs finished with lime render.

The rendered elements were whitewashed using mineral paint to match the appearance of the original tower and unify the whole. The main roof of the extension is planted turf, where the soil from the foundations was set aside and reinstalled upon completion.

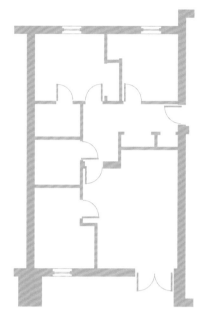

Housing, Brunswick Road, Edinburgh

ISA

BRUNSWICK ROAD IS A former industrial area. The site was previously a Royal Mail sorting office. The existing buildings on Brunswick Road are a mix of ages, types and scales; a listed Victorian primary school, low-volume 1960s housing, tenement gable ends and modern flatted developments.

Previous planning applications for the site had been unsuccessful. The planners were particularly sensitive to the relationship of the proposals to the neighbouring housing estates and street frontage.

ISA responded to this by aligning the proposed buildings with the southern edge of the site to re-define the street, bringing it more in line with the character of the neighbouring Hillside residential area. Edinburgh's New Town has been used as a precedent for the development, with bridges connecting street and building.

The linear blocks are split with landscaped gardens between. These create pedestrian links and permeability through the site from north to south. The landscaped open space to the north of the development provides a buffer to the

neighbours at Allanfield and a green outlook for both the new and old developments.

A simple palette of materials was adopted, with the depth of the balconies being accentuated by the use of dark grey cladding panels. Entrances from the street are framed by white precast concrete surrounds. Blonde brick gives the development a domestic scale. The brick has a natural variation in colour, tonally similar to the traditional tenement sandstone, with texture to add richness to the otherwise simple form.

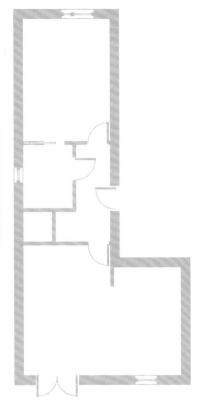

Housing, Magdalene Drive, Edinburgh

ISA

THE DEVELOPMENT AT MAGDALENE Drive consisted of twelve flats and eleven houses for Port of Leith Housing Association and a new church hall for St Martin's Parish Church. The site was formerly occupied by the original St Martin's Church; a 1950s building that was in poor condition and too large for the congregation to manage and maintain.

The project involved demolishing the existing church to provide the congregation with a smaller, more flexible building, better

suited to their requirements. The rest of the site was released for new social housing.

The new church fronts on to Magdalene Drive. Its massing acknowledges the single storey bungalows to the west of the site with the four-storey flats to the east. Large areas of glazing have been provided to maximize daylight and transparency. Sliding timber screens cover the glazing, providing security when the church is closed.

The block of twelve flats terminates the row of four-storey flats that line Magdalene

Drive. The two-storey houses are grouped to the back of the site, relating to the adjacent bungalows. They are organised into terraced blocks to enclose the shared space in the centre of the development. Entrances are set back to create semi-private thresholds.

The development is unified through the use of a limited palette of materials. A multi-hued brick gives the whole development an intimate scale, the colour variation giving richness to the otherwise simple forms.

Garden Room, Trinity, Edinburgh
kalm architecture llp

THIS EXTENSION TO A SUBSTANTIAL stone villa within the Trinity area of Edinburgh provides for a new family space at the back of the house that can be used for living and dining, replacing a late edition bay window and opening up what was an austere relationship between the house and garden into a new, light-filled, threshold space. This new room has two principle elevations: the east façade that follows the existing house geometry and provides a picture window view of the garden as a culmination of the formal enfilade space of the drawing room and the south-east façade which has large glazed doors orientated towards the sun. In doing so it introduces a diagonal movement into the plan and from the kitchen that offers an additional dynamic to the way the house is used.

The project attempts to answer the question of how best to use contemporary, lightweight techniques that both signify a departure from the existing thick masonry construction and yet retain something of the former scale in both the proportions and in the use of thickened pochè wall space. Window seats, storage and bench surfaces become the device used to occupy these thickened walls, thus creating a language of layered internal joinery that sits comfortably in scale with the existing interiors.

The timber and steel framed volume is clad in stained vertical larch weatherboarding with a zinc sloping roof. All the new internal spaces are served by underfloor heating.

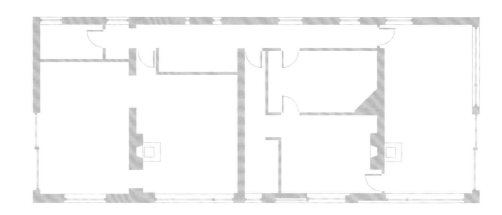

Housing, Portobello, Edinburgh

John Kinsley Architects

TWENTY-SIX BATH STREET is a collective custom-build project. Procuring the building direct by the families who will live in it eliminates the on-costs of a mass housebuilder or private developer and flat costs can be around twenty-percent lower than market rates. The flats are procured as a 'shell and core' allowing a high degree of flexibility in the internal planning and fit-out. This flexibility is maximised by using a cross-laminated timber (CLT) structural frame for the building which requires no internal columns. The CLT frame (currently the largest in Scotland) is exposed on internal walls and ceilings.

Three of the four families involved are current Portobello residents and felt strongly about the building contributing to the local sense of place in Bath Street. The building is carefully integrated into the street by stepping the façade in both section and plan.

Sustainability has been a key driver for the client group; the building is designed to PassivHaus levels of energy efficiency, requiring no central-heating systems. The building will use no fossil fuels and the CLT frame sequesters the equivalent of an average British citizen's carbon-dioxide emissions for ten years. The format of the building follows the traditional Scottish tenement model with a central shared stair providing access not only to each flat but to a shared garden on the roof, with views out seawards over the Forth and inland to Arthur's Seat.

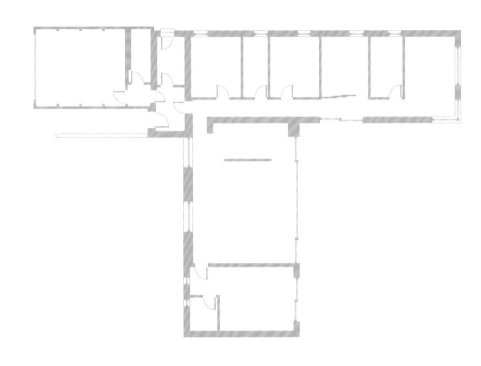

House, Ravelston Dykes Lane, Edinburgh

Konishi Gaffney Architects

THE CLIENTS, WHO WERE retiring from the Far-East back to Edinburgh, had purchased a 1960s bungalow with permission to demolish and build a two-storey house. In discussion and given the desire to build as environmentally-friendly as possible, it was decided that the existing house should be developed and extended to maintain its embodied energy.

The single-storey house with its low, horizontal proportions felt appropriate to this site and the design developed this Japanese sensibility by blending internal and external spaces to connect the house with its large, mature garden. By removing the numerous internal partition walls and opening up the pitched roof, a generous open-plan living space was formed with views through the building from front to back. This space has a new roof structure with expressed scissor trusses and a whitewashed timber ceiling.

A rear extension forms a private bedroom block including a tatami room that opens out onto the south-facing deck. These are connected by a corridor looking out to the garden beyond.

A front door to the lane was formed so that visitors don't walk through the beautiful front garden to reach the main door, helping to enhance its tranquil setting. The existing garage was tied into the house with a new pitched roof with an overhang to create a sheltered external walkway.

The house was insulated externally with high performance insulation and rendered. Triple glazing, a ground-source heat pump, solar photovoltaics and water-recycling sanitaryware all contribute to a strong environmental pedigree.

Photographs © Alan Craigie

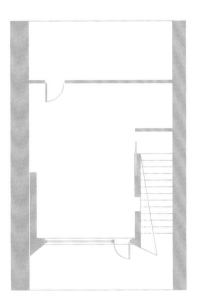

Regent Street Dormer, Portobello, Edinburgh
Konishi Gaffney Architects

THIS PROJECT WAS TO extend a small first floor flat into the loft to form a new bedroom with dormer window. A simple brief, complicated only by the lack of headroom in the loft, the client's design ambition and planning rules in this conservation area.

The street has the densest concentration of listed buildings in Portobello with 54 listed buildings in 120 metres. The planners were resistant to the idea of any dormer in this location. However, following long negotiations, a rear dormer was conceded. The case was made for a long, low-profile dormer, more than twice as long is as normally permitted. It was successfully demonstrated that a single dormer, set back from the eaves had less visual impact than two smaller dormers located at the front of the roof and planning permission was granted.

The dormer forms a west-facing picture window with an unusual view and includes an idiosyncratic splay to allow afternoon light in. The panoramic window is complimented with a timber door for ventilation. The dormer is clad in anthracite zinc to accentuate its angular form. Careful attention was made to the arrangement of the space to maximise usability, with an office area below the new stairs and a bath built into the eaves. The loft extension helped to almost double the available floor space of the house.

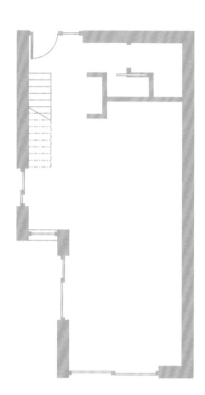

Housing, Juniper Green, Edinburgh
LBA

THE PROJECT IS A RESIDENTIAL development of four, three-storey, five bedroom townhouses. The proposal replaces a disused, single-storey, pitched-roof community hall building that sits on a visually prominent, gently-sloping corner site in the village of Juniper Green on the outskirts of the city of Edinburgh.

The design approach for the proposed townhouses was to provide open-plan, high-quality, contemporary homes. The overall volume of the row of four dwellings is reduced and punctuated by vertical strips of glazed curtain walling between each house bringing light deep into the circulation void that runs up the entire three-storeys of each property. Open-tread timber stairs allow glimpsed views through the buildings out to the south-facing gardens to the rear.

The detailing is simple and crisp with high-quality, durable and timeless materials. The materials palette is a subtle combination of bronze matt-finished aluminium, framed full-height glazing and handmade buff-coloured facing brickwork. Vertical timber-fin screens control privacy and views at both the front entrance area and to the first-floor roof terraces to the rear of the properties. The fin motif and material is echoed in the pergola overhang at the entrance, internal stairs and the boundary fencing / storage units to the landscaped rear garden and terrace.

The houses have excellent environmental credentials with the highly insulated upper flat-roof supporting an array of photovoltaic panels, all concealed from view behind the brickwork parapet.

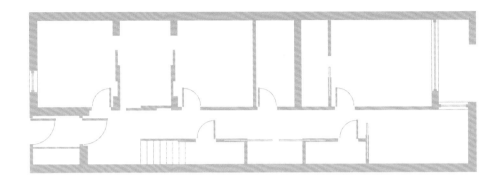

Housing, Liberton, Edinburgh

LBA

THE PROJECT IS A RESIDENTIAL development of three, two-storey, four bedroom townhouses. The existing site comprised a derelict open agricultural barn sat within a collection of previously converted steadings adjacent to the B listed nineteenth century farmhouse. The design approach is a contemporary interpretation of the existing agricultural barn in terms of massing, form and materiality.

An existing stone wall wraps around two sides of the barn. This element is key in defining the building floorplate of the new buildings. The new ground storey stone wall re-imagines the wrapping, protective nature of the existing thick stone wall and also highlights the retaining wall, holding back the sloping site with the new properties tucked in behind it.

The key strategy is to provide open-plan, high-quality, contemporary homes that visually connect with the rural surroundings to the west, whilst maintaining privacy from the surrounding steadings to the east. This privacy has been achieved by wrapping this agricultural form in vertical timber 'hit and miss' cladding. This allows solids and voids/glazing to sit behind the timber, revealing subtle glimpses of what is concealed within.

Due to the long, narrow floor plans the properties have been designed internally around a central, glazed external void courtyard which cuts through both floors of the building. At the first floor level you are exposed to the stunning view west from the large, open-plan, living space with vaulted ceiling.

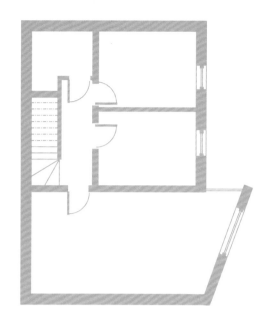

Archers' Hall, The Meadows, Edinburgh
LDN Architects

THIS SENSITIVE ALTERATION AND new-build project creates a new archery butts facility and accommodation for 75 post-graduate students for the University of Edinburgh in the grounds of the Grade A listed Archers' Hall, the home of the Royal Company of Archers. There is a clear separation between the Archers' Hall grounds and the student housing, thus improving the RCA security while avoiding overdeveloping the site with the required four new buildings.

As a means of anchoring the new development to the site, large sections of the existing boundary walls were retained and incorporated into the new buildings whenever possible. The existing cottage lodge was also retained and extended to provide further accommodation.

The new Archery Butts is a flat-roofed, single-storey building clad in untreated oak boards on its garden side, rising over the existing wall to Meadow Lane as a zinc edge. It fulfilled all the sporting requirements of the brief while providing a flexible space for the organisation of events by the RCA.

Set back from the eighteenth century building through a glazed link that allows light to get deep into the plan, the entrance pavilion rises one storey above the existing forecourt wall. It provides an accessible route to both Archers' Hall and the garden. Its zinc-clad flat roof and fully glazed elevations emphasise the distinction between old and new.

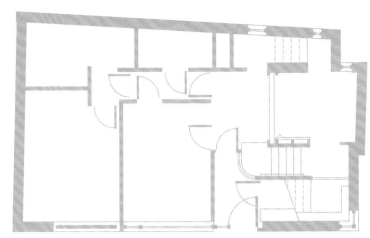

House, New Town, Edinburgh
Richard Murphy Architects

THIS IS A RARE EXAMPLE of the construction of a contemporary house within the World Heritage Site of the New Town of Edinburgh. Designed by Richard Murphy for his own use, it is consequently something of an experiment. Originally recommended for refusal by the local authority planning department, it was given consent by the planning committee.

There are a number of agendas at play. The house maximises the use of a modest area, 165m² on a footprint of only eleven metres by six metres. It has a strong energy agenda and responds to an unresolved corner of the New Town, acting as a 'bookend' to the neighbouring property. Internally a variety of devices transform the spaces from summertime to wintertime use. Finally, the house is a homage to architectural influences, Scarpa, Chareau, Soane, Rietveldt and Frank Lloyd Wright.

Since its completion in December 2014, the *Architect's Journal* named the building their 'House of the Year 2015' and in 2016 it won a Saltire Award for the Best New House in Scotland, a Civic Trust National Award, Edinburgh Architectural Association Building of the Year and was the RIBA/ Channel 4 House of the Year.

Photographs © Keith Hunter Photograpjy

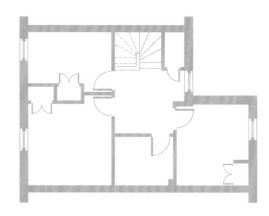

Housing, Dublin Street Lane, Edinburgh
Richard Murphy Architects

THE COMPETITION-WINNING design of this housing in the centre of Edinburgh's New Town is based on the history of the site. Buildings that were demolished sat on the footprint of Broughton village which pre-dated the New Town. The new design preserves the spirit of the original, organically-planned village and is in many ways the antithesis of the order and hierarchy of New Town planning.

The development consists of a walled precinct of houses arranged in two, three-storey, 'ranges' corresponding to previous buildings. The vehicle and pedestrian gates of the precinct are both marked by three-storey gate houses. Most of the development is one and two bedroom flats, except for six family houses on the north side.

In the spirit of reinterpreting the medieval, all apartments are reached by external staircases, living rooms of the top floor flats are placed under the section of the roof with ridge light glazing. All the elevations are freely composed and include timber panels (a memory of the former timber yard nearby) and the spaces between the buildings develop in an equally informal manner.

Housing, Old Fishmarket Close, Edinburgh
Richard Murphy Architects

THIS COMPETITION-WINNING private housing development takes as its inspiration the famous 1647 aerial map of the Old Town of Edinburgh by James Gordon of Rothiemay. The regular sub-division of building fingers of about seven metres has been reproduced, creating two tall, thin, parallel buildings on a steeply sloping site in the Old Town tradition.

Emphasis has been placed on the roof-scape and gable ends which can be viewed at eye level from the Royal Mile. The traditional 'roofed rooms' which have largely disappeared from the Old Town are echoed here, where the exaggerated roofs house spectacular maisonette flats with double-height living spaces. Areas of timber boarding are used at these upper levels, echoing the vernacular timber top storeys of the Old Town and lending the building's scale. The upper gables are largely glazed with a mixture of windows and glass-block to give a lantern-like appearance at night.

The two new buildings are separated by a short and vertiginous new close, which forms an extension of the upper part of Old Fishmarket Close. Both blocks respond to the height of the adjacent Police and Advocates buildings, with the east block book-ending the lower tenement to its north. Underneath the housing, offices and a restaurant have been built into the fall of the site and the original close between the two blocks, long lost, has been resurrected. Started on site in October 2002, the development was completed in January 2004.

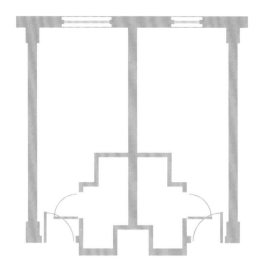

Student Housing, Holyrood, Edinburgh
Oberlanders Architects LLP, jmarchitects and John C Hope Architects

THE HOLYROOD NORTH PROJECT created an international student village within Edinburgh city centre through a unique, historically-contextual response that is of both local and global significance. Located on an extraordinary site in Edinburgh's historic Old Town, the whole development has created over 1,100 new student rooms in a scheme that is strongly rooted in the historic city and enjoys an array of on-site student resources, amenity and social spaces. This project was delivered by a consortium led by Balfour Beatty Construction and their design team of

Oberlanders Architects LLP / jmarchitects and HarrisonStevens Landscape Architects, following a masterplan by John C Hope Architects.

This ground breaking development offers a varied mix of contemporary accommodation for the University of Edinburgh, focused around affordable, residential accommodation targeting international postgraduate and mature undergraduates. A diverse mix of housing types has been configured within a traditional street pattern, from individual apartments and studios, through to a 480

person, communal 'collegiate' self-catering kitchen and dining hall. This hall design is the first of its kind in the UK. At high level, a variety of roof terraces also optimise the wonderful views over the city and act as urban gardens for socialising and relaxing in the sun.

The development has attracted the attention of numerous other universities. Many of them have visited the development and consider it as an exemplar response to student housing within a city context.

199

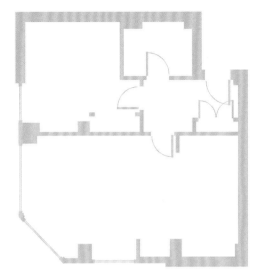

Inglis Point, Edinburgh
Oberlanders Architects LLP

INGLIS POINT IS PIVOTAL to the wider, emerging Springside regeneration masterplan, stitching together previously truncated and unresolved industrial and streetscape interfaces. The peninsular building form, highly visible from three sides, is articulated and suitably scaled to address three distinct elevational conditions.

To the south, a new public realm and community playpark require a civic-scaled frontage. From the north and west, massing and elevational articulation create a distinctive landmark pivotal to both a new pedestrian route from Haymarket to existing and established residential neighbourhoods and to the progression towards the City and its urban context when approached along the Western Approach Road.

The defining characteristics of the building form and massing are its contextual massing, comparable to the adjacent tenements along Upper Grove Place and a strongly-defined podium level to juxtapose and animate the adjacent changes in street level.

From the Western Approach Road to Upper Grove Place a suitably-scaled and civic, south-facing, frontality addresses the new park. An inhabited flank of recessed balconies and terraces are set on the westerly façade. The sculpted form to the upper levels ensures animated vistas from near and far and the palette of bespoke brick bridges the previous industrial context with the colour, hue and texture of existing tenemental stone. Robust materials and forms echo and give memory to the previous industrial context of brewing, kegging and cooperage.

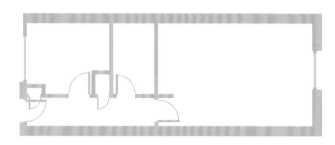

Springside, Edinburgh
Oberlanders Architects LLP

SPRINGSIDE OCCUPIES THE SITE of the historic, though now redundant Fountainbridge brewery, one of the few major industrial sites within the city centre of Edinburgh. The mixed-use urban regeneration creates a contemporary city centre neighbourhood of 650 homes, offices and retail space, with a new park and play area, central to the new network of streets, connecting new and established communities. The first phases have delivered a broad and diverse range of urban apartments for sale, alongside affordable homes for rent, all fully integrated into a cohesive streetscape with a restrained, robust and elegant palette of materials.

To ensure a genuinely diverse community, a wide range of apartment types sit side-by-side, from contemporary urban apartments for first-time buyers, through to homes designed to meet the specific needs of elderly residents. The stated development intent is to create an exemplary new neighbourhood that continues the best traditions of the City's built heritage, but with character and quality representing the best of today.

The traditional tenement streetscape, typical to Edinburgh, had been eroded, cropped and destroyed by the march and expansion of the Fountainbridge brewing industry through previous generations.

The Springside development seeks to reinstate and continue the Edinburgh tradition of a strongly-defined street frontage, today relieved by small pockets of balconies and terraces for residential apartments, mediating between street and dwelling, between civic and private. Animated roofscapes feature discrete outdoor terraces, located to best afford residents fresh air and city views.

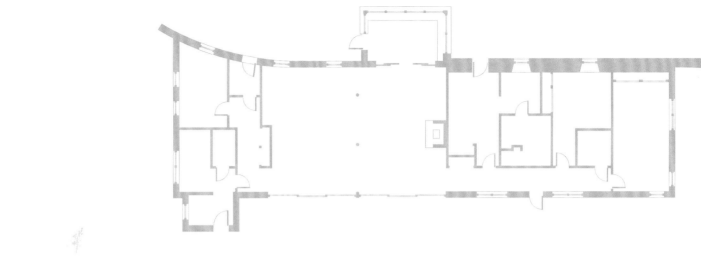

House, Mavisbank Walled Garden, Loanhead

Ian Parsons Architect

BOUNDED TO THE SOUTH by the River North Esk, the oval Walled Garden is enclosed by a three-to-four metre high, listed, brick wall. The new house was part of the restoration of the garden from the tree nursery; with extensive repairs to the walls, gate pillars and steps and three sets of wrought iron gates.

Initial planning approval, for a design by other architects, restricted new development to the site of former potting sheds and this approach was followed for the final design. The single-storey, three bedroom, structure grows from a new, curved extension to the existing brick wall. The pitched roof is separated from the wall by a hidden section of flat roof. Cladding to the, south-facing, private garden is larch and white render, to distinguish new work from original.

The interior contrasts the vaulted kitchen/dining/sitting space with full-height, south-facing windows with the enclosed bedrooms with ceilings and attic above.

Moving from an old house, the owner had intended to sub-divide the main vaulted space. Having lived there for a short period he appreciated the single volume and used only a low level division.

The house is energy efficient with small windows to the north, large areas of south-facing glazing and well-insulated timber-frame construction. The separate energy centre used an existing store, has two solar panels and gives flexibility to change fuel source in the future.

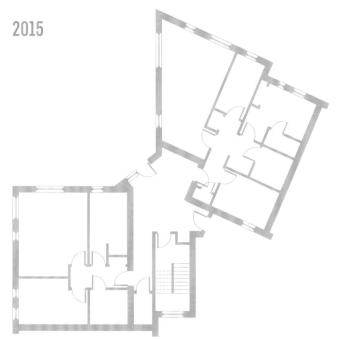

Tudsbery Court, Craigmillar, Edinburgh

Smith Scott Mullan Associates

TUDSBERY COURT IS A mixed tenure development of 73 flats and houses in Craigmillar, south-east Edinburgh, for Places for People. The development is located on a brownfield site in an existing residential area and forms a new edge to the Thistle Foundation Conservation Area. The buildings include a row of two-bedroom terraced houses nestled between three and four-storey flatted blocks. The remainder of the dwellings are dormer cottages assembled on a curve to the west of the site within the East Court of the Thistle Foundation.

A new, landscaped courtyard provides secure, attractive outside spaces for residents to relax and meet. The houses and ground floor flats have small private gardens enclosed by low fencing, with paths leading to seating areas.

Two new pedestrian-orientated streets were constructed with integrated street trees and landscape features including bespoke polished-concrete wall panels to planted areas. The provision of clearly-defined pedestrian connections through the development was an important aspect to enhance the access and permeability for the wider area.

The housing mix is varied, including one, two and three-bedroom apartments and two and three-bedroom houses. All properties are dual aspect and each block provides main-door apartments with direct access from the street. The simple yet mixed palette of materials provides a contemporary finish and forms a connection between the rendered historical houses to the Thistle Foundation and the brick to more recent Greendykes developments.

Tudsbery Court is the second phase of our masterplan with the third and final phase on site in 2017.

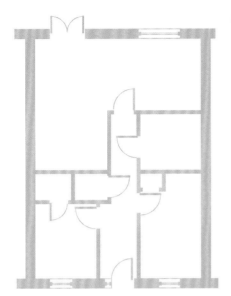

Housing, Gracemount, Edinburgh
Smith Scott Mullan Associates

GRACEMOUNT HOUSING (PHASE ONE) was the first Council housing developed in Edinburgh in twenty years and provided 99 new affordable homes designed within the context of an existing masterplan in place of existing unsuccessful tower blocks. The development includes a rich mixture of flats, houses, main-door flats and colony houses, many incorporating enhanced design and space standards for families. All homes feature increased ceiling heights and there are eleven wheelchair-accessible units to the ground floor.

A central street was formed on the axis of the listed Gracemount House, with pedestrian connections formed north/ south. The rich building form creates a group of four-storey buildings around the central street, reducing to two and three-storey buildings towards the edges of the site, enhanced with an ordered brickwork elevation treatment throughout.

The principle of the open space design was to provide a variety of spaces including private gardens, balconies, shared open space and public open space to the north

of Gracemount House. The design of the streets was in accordance with the Scottish Government planning policy, 'Designing Streets', creating a high-quality environment where the public realm is safely shared between vehicles and people.

The project complied with the City of Edinburgh Council's Residential Design Standards, Sustainable Building Standards, Housing for Varying Needs and achieved Secured by Design and Eco Homes Excellent accreditation. The completed homes were occupied in 2012.

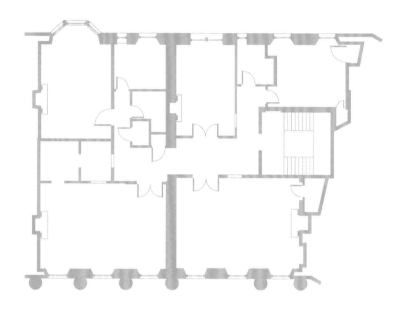

Moray Place, Edinburgh

Somner Macdonald Architects

MORAY PLACE IS A BEAUTIFUL Georgian circus, made up of fine and grand houses overlooking a central garden. It's scale is imposing, the openness striking and the quality of the buildings impressive.

We were challenged to create one of the most distinctive apartments in Edinburgh. The starting point was compromised – a property spanning across the first floors of two townhouses. These properties had been altered unsympathetically, on numerous occasions, during the early 1900s and they were in a mess.

A huge amount of effort went into research – understanding the history of the property, how it had been sub-divided and altered and where walls and features had once existed. We worked hard to reinstate some original features and proportions, particularly the front rooms which would have spanned the full three-windowed width of each townhouse.

The plan that we ended with is simple, reflecting the scale and formality of the original. With the front of the property facing west, large openings were formed between the front day spaces and the rear bedrooms, to allow light to flood deep into the footprint of the property. The sense of openness, connection and spaciousness is strong. The style of the finishes – classic, simple, unfussy – creates a cohesive apartment, which feels modern, yet respectful. Services were designed for efficiency and materials used sparingly. The end result is transformational.

House, Craiglockhart, Edinburgh
Studio DuB

THE SITE WAS PURCHASED with planning consent for a humdrum suburban detached house. The new design approach retained the eaves and ridge height to ease passage through planning, but totally reworked the design, leaving nothing but the silhouette.

Inside, the standard, two-storey, arrangement has been transformed into three levels including a ready-made loft conversion. The steel ring-beam maximises the volume, allowing a mezzanine to engage with the living area whilst supporting the roof above.

An overgrown dormer cantilevers to the front face, punctuating the entrance, whilst the living area provides sightlines right through the main volume. This house reinvents a tired suburban typology, creating a crisply-detailed, welcoming new home.

Natural materials were used extensively inside, including eco-paints and natural oak flooring above the underfloor heating panels. Recycled railway sleepers form the retaining wall to the terraced garden to the rear. The 'slate' cladding is man-made but achieves a very good rating for energy efficiency and sustainability (fibre cement is also a 100% recyclable building material). Painted timber doors and windows were made locally, using timber from sustainably managed resources. The dormers are zinc-clad.

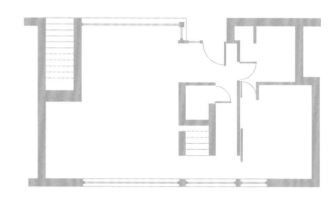

West Burn Lane, St Andrews

Sutherland Hussey Harris

WEST BURN LANE RUNS north to south linking South Street and Queen's Terrace. The lane comprises a mix of residential properties of varying character, style and scale, dominated by the eastern facade of the University of St Andrews' Bute building. The site sits on the east side of the lane and gently slopes down from north to south.

The project was the subject of limited competition in 2012. It consists of fourteen unique dwellings of varying sizes. The site is sub-divided into nine plots, each contain a free standing building. These in turn contai one, two or four dwellings, each varying from its adjacent neighbour, echoing the historical development of the old riggs of Scottish market towns. There are seven house types within three broad typologies descending down the lane.

The townhouses are three-storey, four bedroom stand-alone houses in a rhythmic street pattern of narrow-frontage, deep-plan and wide-frontage, thin-plan with private gardens, garages, flexible living spaces and roof terraces. The maisonettes are interlocked within three-storey buildings, set back from a courtyard space, providing a mix of two and three bedroom units with either private gardens or terraces. The largest block at four storeys offers a range of apartments with vistas over the surrounding hills and countryside to the south.

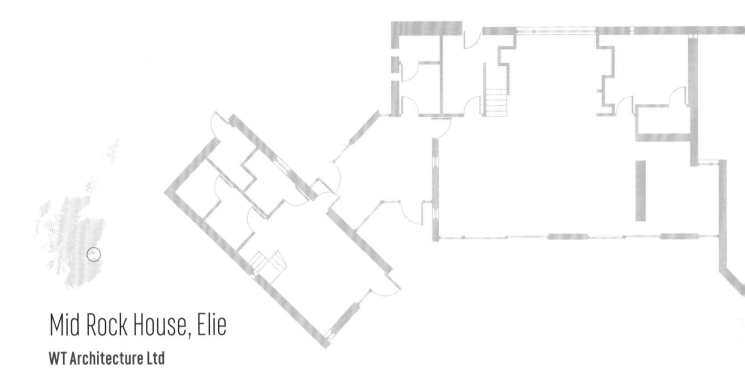

Mid Rock House, Elie
WT Architecture Ltd

THIS BEACH-SIDE HOUSE replaces a 1970s bungalow with a house that engaged with its dramatic coastal location and aims to enable its occupants to luxuriate in the special views over the Firth of Forth. The building form is broken into parts to tie it in with the scale and massing of its vernacular neighbours. An open plan living space with a horizontal, sedum-covered, roof links the two-storey main house to the small bothy accommodation.

The main entrance to the house from the landward side is between the two main sections of the house, which frame a view through to a lighthouse on the far side of the beach. The living space linking the larger, two-storey, main house to the bothy accommodation is largely glazed, with open-plan sitting, dining and TV spaces. First-floor bedrooms look out over the sedum roof, bringing the landscape right up to the window sills, emphasising a closeness to the sea when the tide is in.

By contrast the landward side is deliberately more closed down and protects the privacy of the house.

A palette of timber boarding and zinc was chosen to reflect the feel of sea-side boatsheds. Wrapping zinc roof planes and timber-boarded screens sit on and inside heavier whitewashed masonry walls, which also extend away from the house to create pockets of shelter and privacy on what is a very public site. Internal materials are simple and utilitarian.

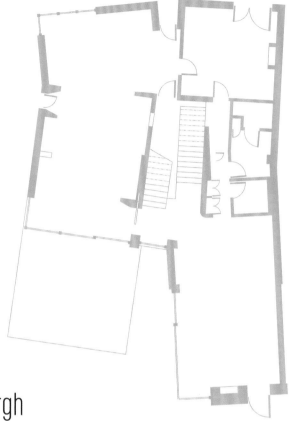

The Old Schoolyard, Wester Coates, Edinburgh
ZONE Architects

THE OLD SCHOOLYARD IS A new villa in a conservation area just west of Edinburgh's city centre.

The ambition was to create a contemporary home which matched the scale and grandeur of its neighbours, substantial Victorian villas in an established suburb. Sited with an open, front garden which directly addresses the street, the building creates a meaningful relationship with both its immediate neighbours and the wider locale.

The stone, cubic form of the house has been conceptually distorted and then split to allow light deep into the stairwell at the centre of the plan and down to the north facing front door on the lower ground floor. A restrained palette of high quality materials frame a range of sun filled living spaces which directly address the south facing garden. A starting point for imagining the form of the building was the recollection of the scale, weight and effort of extraction of a large block of hewn stone fresh from

a quarry, a recollection of the tradition and history of stone quarrying essential to the construction of much of Edinburgh.

Internally the accommodation is spread over three floors with service/garage/swimming pool on the lower ground level, living spaces and rooms on the ground, garden level and four bedrooms on the upper level. A variety of both open-plan and cellular rooms is offered, as a reflection of the complexities and changing needs of contemporary family life.

Photographs © Paul Zanre

Central Belt: West

For Glasgow the challenge over recent decades has been to replace the historic tenemental landscape and the tower blocks which followed, with attractive homes which would rebuild communities and draw people back into the city. Elegant new tenements maintain the urban scale in the centre, stepping down to more modest blocks and terraces on the periphery. Both scales are well represented here, alongside clever adaptations and individual dwellings within the wide and varied landscape of the West.

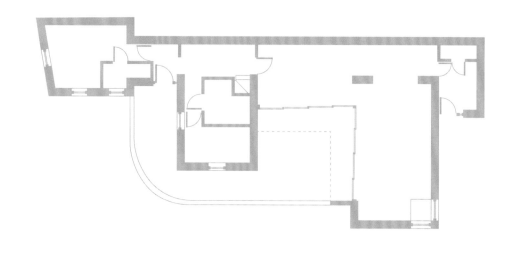

The Coach House, Falkirk

:thatstudio chartered architects ltd

SET WITHIN THE ARNOTHILL and Dollar Park Conservation area and conceived as an 'inside-outside' dwelling this grouping of three pavilions is arranged around a series of courtyards, 'entrance, heart and back green.' The entrance court allows the existing buildings to command their own setting, whilst the central courtyard provides focus and allows the living spaces to double in size when the large glazed doors are opened. A cantilevered canopy projection provides shelter, allowing the big glass doors to be opened when the weather is warm, but wet. The back green is a quieter, private space. Glazing is placed to capture light at specific times of day in parallel with usage patterns to deliver maximum natural illumination with minimal glare.

The pavilions are small and cellular lending themselves to becoming bedroom and study spaces, providing a cosier, intimate environment. The third new pavilion takes its architectural form from the gabled character of the context and maximises use of its volume to create a lofty living space. All three pavilions are connected by a single storey link, to function as a single dwelling. Heat and hot water is captured from the ground via a ground-source heat pump, feeding the whole house underfloor heating system and providing hot water too, negating any need for a gas supply.

The materials palette is restrained. The existing has received like-for-like repair and conservation whilst the new additions combine ashlar stonework, zinc, slate and aluminium framed glazing.

231

Photographs © Keith Hunter Photography

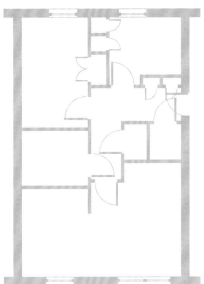

Housing, Duke Street / High Street, Glasgow
Anderson Bell Christie

THE DEVELOPMENT OF 46 energy-efficient modern homes around a private garden has rejuvenated an unused part of land within walking distance of the city centre. The site stretches up over a steep slope from the thoroughfare of Duke Street to the ancient High Street. This presented a major architectural and building challenge. The site also lies in the shadow of Glasgow Cathedral in the city's historic core. The city's planners insisted that every detail should be sensitive to the character and heritage of the area.

High Street is one of the few remaining medieval streets in Glasgow and leads from the cathedral to the city centre. The development is on part of the site of Duke Street prison, which closed in 1955 and was demolished a few years later. The land has been largely unused since the 1970s with the surrounding area in decline. The new homes have breathed new life into the area and helped Glasgow Housing Association increase the range of homes available for rent.

The city centre location and its proximity to excellent transport links created an opportunity to build an attractive, car-free, development which suited potential tenants' lifestyles. Areas that might have been used for car parking were reserved for communal green spaces. This approach has proved successful as tenants are delighted to have homes in a well-connected, central location which does not necessitate the use of a car, resulting in a significantly reduced carbon footprint for the development.

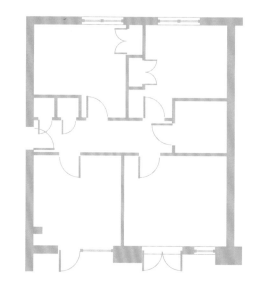

Housing, Fernan Gardens, Glasgow

Anderson Bell Christie

THE KEY AIMS OF THE project were to provide amenity housing (social-let properties for age 55+) for Shettleston Housing Association. The development was designed to include 29 units with two wheelchair accessible. The homes incorporate a number of design features aimed at enhancing the quality of life for the new residents, particularly the shared common courtyard, offering the residents space to socialise. The ground floor residents enjoy a private terrace with raised planting beds, built at a height to make them convenient for accessing the beds.

The site sits at a prominent corner, at the junction of Old Shettleston Road and Fernan Street. Our approach to the site was to have the blocks set back from the footpaths (following the pattern of surrounding residential buildings) to create a landscaped buffer zone to the road-side, whilst providing a safe, enclosed private courtyard. There is a simple but robust elevational treatment with high quality brick and large 'Juliet' balcony windows with frameless glass balustrading. These repeat in a rhythm, with closes highlighted with a higher parapet wall.

There is one principal pedestrian entrance from Fernan Street via a covered pend to the courtyard from where the properties are accessed. There is also parking available for thirteen, with two of these spaces allocated for wheelchair users. It is anticipated that this two-storey development will complete the immediate area, contributing to the wider regeneration of Shettleston.

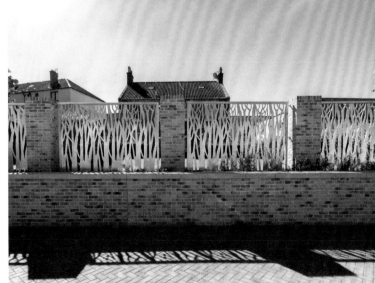

2014

Housing, Maybole
Austin-Smith:Lord LLP

THE THIRTEEN PROPERTIES AT Burns Wynd, Maybole, were designed to take maximum benefit from the steeply-sloping site and rural setting. Designed as a staggered terrace, each unit has private entrance courts and garden spaces to maximise privacy and the open views towards the Southern Uplands. Nine two-bedroom and four three-bedroom homes are each designed to accommodate a range of needs by ensuring that all have downstairs bedrooms and bathrooms.

The steep slope made road access into the site difficult. It was decided to utilise narrow frontage, deep-plan houses, leaving the remote south corner of the site for landscaping. The change in level across the site is such that each house steps up the slope. The majority of houses are two bedroom, designed with hall, kitchen, bathroom and lounge in a deep-plan, pitched-roof, wing linked to the adjacent house with a shallow, pitch-roofed, bedroom wing. This emphasises the individual houses and the shallow pitch-link accommodates the changes in floor level.

The larger, three bedroom, houses have two of the three bedrooms at first-floor level. These are used architecturally as a stop-end to the terrace. They also accentuate the breaks in the terrace to accommodate pedestrian access points to the rear of the properties. The variation in depth between the living room-kitchen wing and the bedroom wing provides a double-height, south-facing, lounge and sheltered rear garden sitting area, whilst the front entrance court is overlooked by a north-facing kitchen.

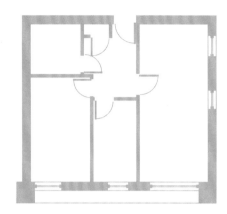

Housing, Govan, Glasgow
Austin-Smith:Lord LLP

THE DEVELOPMENT SITS WITHIN a tight site in the Govan conservation area, surrounded by Grade A listed buildings and adjacent to former ship-building yards. A compact plan accommodates the brief for 27 flats with 69 bed spaces.

The apartments occupy the full footprint of the site. Therefore only the street-facing north and west elevations can accommodate habitable rooms. This is to their advantage however, as all these rooms are afforded views across the Clyde to the new Riverside Museum. Common areas, stairs, lifts and circulation spaces are located on the south elevation where windows have been recessed from the boundary to allow sun to penetrate into small sitting areas.

While it is recognised that most elderly residents tend to prefer internal spaces, a south-facing external roof garden, in the form of a loggia, provides a sun-trap sitting space for those wishing to sit out on sunny days. Additional external amenity space is provided by a balcony over the roof garden. Both areas have proven to be intensely-utilised social spaces.

The external envelope is highly insulated and combines thermal mass in concrete floors with block walls to retain solar-gain. The fenestration of the seven storey flats is grouped 2:3:2 to relate to that of the adjacent, 19th century, former YMCA. The facing brick was carefully selected to reflect the common brick of the existing back courts and Govan's rich industrial heritage.

243

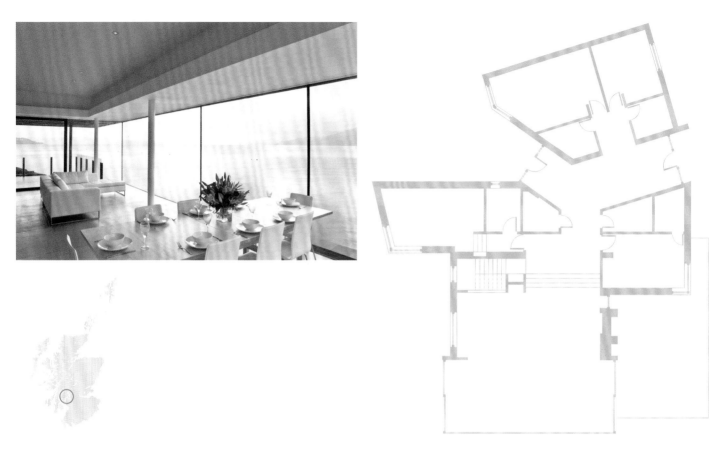

Cape Cove, Helensburgh

cameronwebster architects

A NAVAL OUTLOOK POST WAS built during the second world war on this spectacular site, right at the water's edge, with a view across Loch Long and straight down the Firth of Clyde. It had been converted into a small house some time previously, but this had not taken the opportunity that the site offered.

While the main body and roof of the existing building was retained, the elevation facing the water was extended with full-height frameless glazing. The garage and accommodation at the entrance was reorganised to provide five bedrooms and a spacious living, dining and kitchen area that takes full advantage of the view. The external terrace is partly covered to provide a heated barbecue area. A hot tub is also positioned to enjoy the prospect down the loch.

The arrival sequence was considered in both a practical sense and as an aesthetic control of the big view. The degagement at the entrance offers a pause and threshold to the main house and articulates the private and service areas. Throughout the house, the materials are detailed to allow a distinction between the surface you touch and the opening towards big views as well as more intimate, close views.

House, Lenzie

cameronwebster architects

THE EXISTING HOUSE, WHICH was built in the middle of the last century, had rather small rooms but a large mature garden, sloping up to the south. The client required a more open-plan living arrangement with a better connection to the garden.

The rear of the house was extended to the south, raising the floor to the level of the existing lawn, with an open-planned series of spaces to accommodate the client's lifestyle. The entry sequence was reorganised to incorporate a double-height hall and the threshold to the new stair and private areas of the house. A large master bedroom was built on top of the existing garage.

The new additions are articulated externally using bronze cladding. This will patinate to represent a rich and robust contrast to the white render of the existing.

Internally the timber linings wrap around the hallway and up the stair, invoking a warmth and connection between the existing and new spaces.

Daylight is brought into the new spaces from above, to catch the soft Scottish light at different times of day and animate the wall surfaces surrounding the hall, dining and living areas.

247

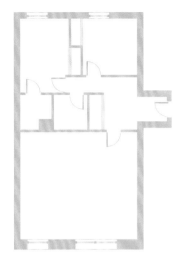

The Bridge, Argyle Street, Glasgow
CMM Architects

GLASGOW'S FIRST CONTEMPORARY high rise to address a whole city block in an uncompromisingly uniform manner, the economics of this project required a free commercial ground plate with a single secure, concierged access point to the 165 flats above. This brief drove the development of half a city block within Glasgow's central gridiron.

Along with 100% underground parking was a desire for apartments that were suitable for contemporary city life: suitable for rent; sharing young professionals and short term ownerships. This was the targeted model, manifest in the quality of entrance slate walls, limestone floors and highly finished bathroom pods.

Success can be judged by this development still being regarded as the most commercially sustainable housing in the area. Architecturally the building reflects this programme. A single grand entrance leads up to a landscaped court, giving access via six stair/lift cores – to eleven floors of apartments. A solid block raised on a colonnade, two storeys high, encloses two storeys of glazed commercial space.

The housing element, like the massive stone buildings of the gridiron, has a substantial presence, a rainscreen 600mm thick and, like solid masonry, deep-framed windows perforate in a simple repeating pattern. Mirroring the base, the wall culminates in a brise-soleil screening recessed two-storey penthouses.

The uniform terracotta relates to the red sandstone of Argyle Street with the deep recesses giving a high degree of modelling to the façade. Unlike other contemporary inner city structures the building has weathered well and remains an imposing street presence.

Housing, Anderston, Glasgow
Collective Architecture

THE ANDERSTON AREA OF central Glasgow underwent significant changes in the 1960s as a result of comprehensive redevelopment. Victorian tenements that once lined this section of Argyle Street were replaced with system-built concrete flats, which ignored the original street pattern. This development, for Sanctuary Scotland Housing Association, consists of 44 flats, five townhouses and a commercial unit.

The design strategy for the development focuses on the creation of a contemporary tenement building arranged around closes, or communal stairs, with two or three flats per floor, creating smaller groups of neighbours at each floor level and within each stair well.

A retail unit to the east addresses an important civic corner within the overall masterplan. The other corners are inhabited by a church, the housing association's own offices and an arts centre. The corner also leads to a wide pedestrian route, which connects the development into the wider regeneration area.

The building employs a simple approach to issues of sustainability, with large windows to the south and small windows to the north, simple, well sourced, materials, robust detailing and good levels of insulation throughout, rather than device oriented energy solutions. In the wider sense of sustainability, the building is successfully supporting a thriving existing community, is well-loved and appreciated, all of which should help to ensure the building's longevity.

House, Dunblane
Denholm Partnership

THIS FAMILY HOME WAS designed to make the most of its stunning location overlooking Dunblane. The main living spaces open up to the garden and views beyond, bringing the outside and daylight in all year round. Covered verandas and entrance areas not only provide shelter from the climate but allow the family to make use of the outdoor spaces as an extension of the house.

The exterior materials reflect the rural setting, a traditional mix of stone, timber and slate, all of which are robust enough to deal with the site's exposure and to stand the test of time. In order to respond to the setting of this unique site we felt it was important to have a more private, traditionally-proportioned stone elevation facing the existing public access track to the east.

On the opposing side of the house and to maximise the uninterrupted views of Dunblane, we developed a more contemporary response, using modern materials such as zinc cladding and larger areas of glass. This allows the house to sit comfortably within its setting whilst also providing a well-balanced internal flow with some open-plan spaces alongside more traditional internal spaces.

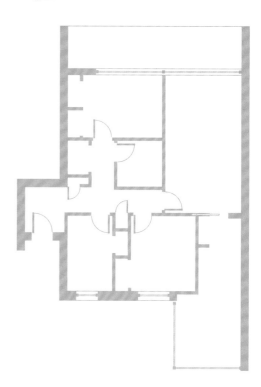

Housing, Laurieston, Glasgow

Elder and Cannon

THIS SUBSTANTIAL NEW residential development of affordable housing is located just south of the Clyde in Glasgow's Laurieston area. As the first phase of a comprehensive redevelopment it establishes a new urban grain through the creation of a pattern of streets, courtyard gardens, squares and mews-type places which reference the historic urban character of the area.

At the southern edge of the masterplan a gateway pavilion block is a re-interpretation of the traditional Glasgow tenement. In that tradition the cohesive block form is composed of a diverse range of dwelling types, including apartments, maisonettes and some three-storey extended family townhouses.

The development was designed and composed to maintain the continuity and restraint which characterises 'tenemental living', while introducing the specific client requirement that all dwellings should have a garden, terrace or balcony forming a private open air space. These are interpreted in response to particular site conditions. Ground floor living spaces which face the street are offered recessed terraces for additional privacy. Corners are highlighted as important, the proximity of an active railway line prompted the creation of a shared common courtyard in place of the traditional corner.

As the new community takes shape and the landscape matures, the rigour of the architecture recedes and is defined by the personality of the people living there. Small interventions and exhibitions of belongings on balconies and terraces mark these places as an important part of people's daily lives and an integral and well used extension to their homes.

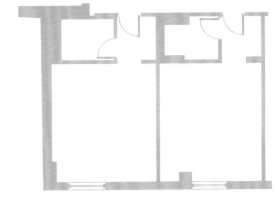

St Aloysius Residence, Garnethill, Glasgow
Elder and Cannon

SITUATED WITHIN A SENSITIVE urban context the building organises a range of spaces and volumes to cater for ten unrelated adults to interact as a community. It also provides for their private, working and spiritual needs within a rich and non-institutional environment. The building contains two functions. At the ground floor are community services with offices, conference and counselling facilities, accessed from a small protected courtyard off the gable elevation.

Above ground is the residence for ten priests and their guests, occupying three floors. The key communal facilities are located on the second floor where dining and kitchen functions are accessed from a double volume reception space. The reception area also links to a, top-lit, prayer room. This is expressed as a tall timber element to the rear of the building. The floor above houses a small library and the main living space which interconnects with a south facing terrace, partially screened from the street by a colonnade.

Interspersed throughout the floors are private bedrooms and break-out spaces which add variation to the living and social possibilities. The building is organised throughout to add volumetric interest and targeted natural light. This building acts as a home, a retreat and place of work for the community of priests who occupy it while also enriching the tenemental urban landscape within which it sits.

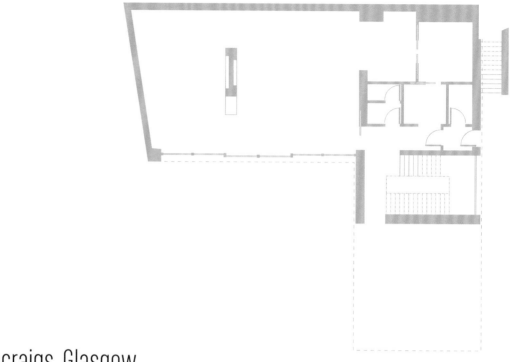

TrägerHaus, Whitecraigs, Glasgow
HAUS Collective

ON THE PERIPHERY OF THE Upper Whitecraigs conservation area of Glasgow, TrägerHaus unifies the traditional aesthetic of its context with an ambition to create a dynamic and reactive architecture that exists in sympathy with its site. A conventional, pitched volume continues the domestic street edge of its context, concealing behind it a cascading form that exploits the dramatically sloping topography of its site. The footprint of the house is polite at ground level, enveloped by an expansive paved veranda that translates into a large capacity driveway when the inhabitants wish to entertain.

Upon approach to the front door, the ground falls away to reveal the form of the architecture emerging below. Visitors are received into a, bottom-lit, circulation area, drawing them down to the main living space where a free plan, walled with glass, interconnects the substantial kitchen, dining and living spaces with the terrace and gardens below.

A cantilever extends the master bedroom above, affording it with elevated south-easterly views across the links and seclusion from the rest of the house.

The ancillary sleeping accommodation lies at the lowest level of the house, burrowed and protected within the gardens. Each bedroom has a presence of its own, opened to the grounds beyond through a sliding wall of glazing that offers direct access. A sauna adds an additional element of luxury and enjoyment for the inhabitants.

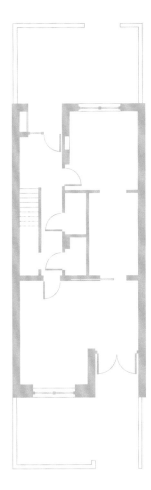

Terraced Housing, West End, Glasgow
Hoskins Architects

IN 2013 A FEASIBILITY STUDY was undertaken for Partickhill Bowling Club which sits within a largely Victorian settlement in Glasgow's West End. The brief was around exploring options to revitalise the Bowling Club's clubhouse and grounds. In order to provide funds to improve its facilities, the Club decided to release an unused area of the grounds for development.

Set in the heart of Glasgow's historic West End conservation area, the Hillside Gardens Lane development comprises six townhouses and associated gardens for the client, Noah Developments. The scheme is composed of a linear terraced block, which forms a transition between the existing surrounding tenements and the villas/mews buildings.

The building completes the unfinished urban block, enclosing and framing the existing bowling green and the clubhouse pavilion building. The scheme uses a limited palette of high-quality materials – predominantly brick. The façade is articulated by a series of bays and has large, vertically-oriented, openings with deep reveals, which evoke the solidity of the surrounding tenements.

The landscaped gardens act as a buffer between the houses and the bowling green and create a new communal space that is shared between the residents of the townhouses and the Bowling Club members.

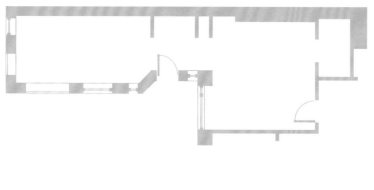

The Collector's House, Pollokshields, Glasgow
Loader & Monteith Architects

AT THE HEART OF THE aspiration for the internal reconfiguration of this flat within a villa in Pollokshields was forming a convivial kitchen around which family life would orbit.

The clients produced a brief for us at the outset which included evocative images which spoke of warmth, material-tactility and honesty in how they were used. In response, a simple palette of lacquered painted MDF and softwood, concrete, reclaimed beech and birch veneered ply was used.

On visiting the property, the kitchen seemed a long way away from the remainder of the living spaces. It was contained within a dark, linear garden projection, which was ironic, given it had potential for more windows, rooflights and an enhanced roof volume – almost unheard of within Glasgow flats. The dining room was redundant and there was a convoluted entrance to it from the hall.

The kitchen was pulled into the centre of the property, forming a new access directly from the hall (which facilitated the formation of a larder) and differentiated between the two living rooms in the property – one for the evenings which was contained within the heart of the flat and a day room within the existing garden projection. Roof ties were exposed and a new roof light introduced to fill the room with light. All the windows serving the spaces were adapted in the process.

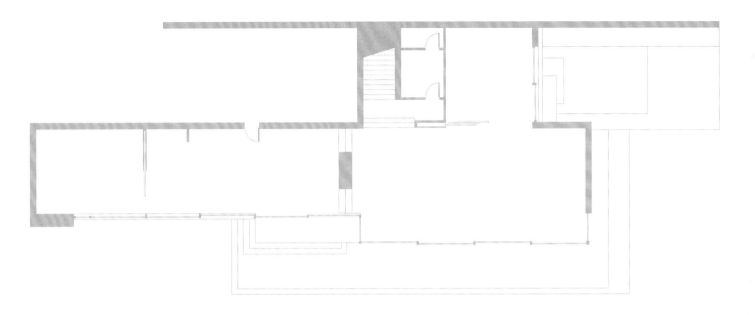

House, Rhu, Helensburgh

McInnes Gardner Architects

THIS PROJECT WAS TO refurbish a 1970s self-built house, on the hillside at Shandon, Rhu, overlooking the Gareloch. The client sought a minimalist and striking twenty-first century home, founded upon the principles of the original house upgraded to the most modern standards and reflecting their own lifestyle, tastes and travel experiences, particularly referencing Japanese design.

The existing link stair between the two wings needed replaced. This gave the opportunity to build a new, over-sailing, upper wing creating a purpose-built viewing gallery facing the Gareloch and mountains beyond. The lower wing needed to be increased in size to accommodate a larger lounge. With full-height, floor-to-ceiling, glazing along the entire west elevation on the lower wing, a new steel structure was required, which in turn supports the new gallery 'pod' above.

The building has a strong horizontal orientation consisting of dark glazing bands, strong white-rendered fascia elements and areas of geometrically-patterned concrete-relief panels.

The building's design language references Frank Lloyd Wright's Falling Water and his Ennis House in the use of layering and texture. The horizontal trays are earthed and visually pinned to the ground by the single vertical element of the chimney which hangs, mid-space, above the open fireplace in the lounge and separates the lounge and dining areas.

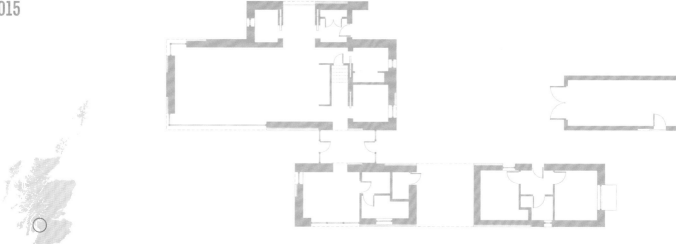

Newhouse of Auchengree, North Ayrshire
Ann Nisbet Studio

THIS CONTEMPORARY FARMHOUSE, sensitively draws on the inherent characteristics of North Ayrshire's unique rural vernacular. The building reflects the identity of the area, creating a sense of place in both the site and wider landscape. Set in a prominent, elevated position and surrounded by agricultural fields, the house is deeply rooted in its context. The building is a cluster of separate spaces, reflecting the way that rural buildings were developed and extended over decades past.

Arrival is via a long access road, entering through a pend into an internal courtyard, thus creating a threshold between the house and the landscape. The composition of the courtyard controls the elements, captures views and mediates between the scale of the surroundings and the intimate scale of the dwelling. The main public spaces and bedrooms are set within a two-storey section. The master bedroom is set within a linear single-storey area and there is an annex, with a further two bedrooms. The whole composition clusters around a three-sided courtyard to the east and a sheltered terrace to the south-west.

The buildings are connected by a route that runs from north to south, flowing through and connecting both the south/west courtyard, the internal courtyard, the outbuilding and orchard, at each stage framing views of the landscape. The building is clad in zinc, providing a contemporary exterior that references; the local agricultural buildings and the foundries once prevalent in the area.

Photographs © David Barbour

Photographs above and opposite lower left © David Barbour
Photographs opposite page top and lower right © Susan Castillo

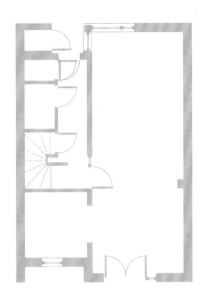

Housing, Penilee, Glasgow
Riach Partnership Ltd

SITUATED IN GLASGOW'S south-western suburb of Penilee, this, new-build, residential development was undertaken on behalf of Southside Housing Association. The project is located on the corner of Gleddoch and Craigmuir Road, a site formally occupied by a post-war, mixed-use, building comprising deck-access flats set over ground floor retail. Penilee – originally developed as a housing scheme during the 1930s – has recently been subject to comprehensive redevelopment with large areas of new housing.

The brief was for family houses and a mixture of one and two bedroom flats, all of which were to meet current housing for varying needs and secured by design standards and achieve an EcoHomes "very good" rating. Through consultation with the housing association, the development was conceived as a terrace of six family townhouses and a block of nine flats.

The intention of the design was to create a block containing the flats which gave prominence to the street corner, whilst mediating the change in scale and character between Gleddoch and Craigmuir roads.

The two-storeyed terraced houses each have four bedrooms and private gardens to the front and rear, complete with in-curtilage parking. The flats are contained within a three-storey block and are a mixture of one and two bedroom units, arranged around a communal close with a shared garden to the rear.

281

Are you considering transforming your property?

The RIAS Clients Advisory Service can help you to select an
architect for your project – contact info@rias.org.uk.

The RIAS Directory of Architectural Practices provides
information on Scotland's architects and the many projects
they have worked on, from housing extensions to multi-million
pound developments. Go to www.rias.org.uk/directory.

Sign up to Architect in the Hoose and
speak to an architect for ideas and inspiration.
Visit www.hoose.scot.

You may also wish to contact any of the practices
featured in this book directly.

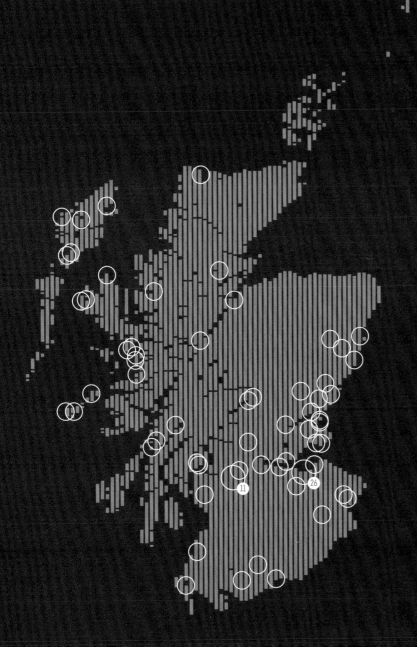

Index of Architectural Practices

230

:thatstudio chartered architects ltd

100 High Street

Linlithgow EH49 7AQ

+44 (0) 1506 201463

mail@thatstudio.scot

www.thatstudio.scot

14

Anderson Associates Chartered Architects Ltd

Harbour View, Cromwell Street Quay

Stornoway

Isle of Lewis HS1 2DF

+44 (0) 1851 701500

architect@andersonassociatesltd.com

www.andersonassociatesltd.com

16   244   246

cameronwebster architects

The Printworks

10 Otago Street

Glasgow G12 8JH

+44 (0) 141 330 9898

mail@cameronwebster.com

www.cameronwebster.com

146

Chambers McMillan Architects

9e Bellfield Lane

Portobello

Edinburgh EH15 2BL

+44 (0) 131 669 5766

ian@chambersmcmillan.com

www.chambersmcmillan.com

138

7N Architects

7 Randolph Place

Edinburgh EH3 7TE

+44 (0) 131 220 5541

info@7narchitects.com

www.7narchitects.com

234   236

Anderson Bell Christie

382 Great Western Road

Glasgow G4 9HT

+44 (0) 141 339 1515

gen@andersonbellchristie.com

www.andersonbellchristie.com

144

Capital A Architecture Ltd

8 Cameron Drive

Falkland

Fife KY15 7DL

+44 (0) 131 208 2075

project@capitala.co.uk

www.capitala.co.uk

120   122

Oliver Chapman Architects

36 St Mary's Street

Edinburgh EH1 1SX

+44 (0) 131 477 4513

admin@oliverchapmanarchitects.com

www.oliverchapmanarchitects.com

118   140

A449 Architects

266-268 Portobello High Street

Edinburgh EH15 2AT

+44 (0) 131 563 5152

mj@a449.co.uk

www.a449.co.uk

240   242

Austin-Smith:Lord LLP

296 St Vincent Street

Glasgow G2 5RU

+44 (0) 141 223 8500

glasgow@austinsmithlord.com

www.austinsmithlord.com

18   20

CASA

Treetops

Dull

Aberfeldy

Perthshire PH15 2JQ

+44 (0) 1887 820 815

colin@casarchitect.co.uk

www.casarchitect.co.uk

250

CMM Architects

81 St Vincent Street

Glasgow G2 5TF

+44 (0) 141 204 4498

admin@cmmarchitects.co.uk

www.cmmarchitects.co.uk

22

26 30

34 38 40

150

Colin Smith + Judith Wilson : Architects

The Laundry Studio

Ethie, Inverkeilor

Arbroath DD11 5SP

+44 (0) 1241 830372

architects@csjwa.co.uk

www.csjwa.co.uk

Denizen Works

29 Wadeson Street

London E2 9DR

+44 (0) 20 3696 6900

info@denizenworks.com

www.denizenworks.com

Dualchas Architects Ltd

Fàs Building

Sabhal Mor Ostaig

Sleat

Isle of Skye IV44 8RQ

+44 (0) 1471 833 300

info@dualchas.com

www.dualchas.com

EMA Architecture + Design Ltd

42 Charlotte Square

Edinburgh EH2 4HQ

+44 (0) 131 247 1450

info@ema-architects.co.uk

www.ema-architects.co.uk

24 124 252

32

42

46

Collective Architecture

Top Floor

Mercat Building

26 Gallowgate

Glasgow G1 5AB

+44 (0) 141 552 3001

info@collectivearchitecture.co.uk

www.collectivearchitecture.co.uk

Professor Gokay Deveci FRIAS RIBA, Chartered Architect

The Sir Ian Wood Building

Robert Gordon University

Riverside East

Garthdee Road

Aberdeen AB10 7GJ

g.deveci@rgu.ac.uk

edge Architecture & Design

Hillview

167 Findhorn

Forres IV36 3YL

+44 (0) 1309 691408

studio@edgearchitecture.co.uk

www.edgearchitecture.co.uk

Fearn Macpherson Chartered Architects

Unit 4

Dunkeld Road

Aberfeldy PH15 2AQ

+44 (0) 1887 820 098

rob.macpherson@fearnmacpherson.com

www.fearnmacpherson.com

256

126

258 262

152

Denholm Partnership

11 Dunira Street

Comrie PH6 2LJ

+44 (0) 1764 670 899

admin@james-denholm.co.uk

www.denholmpartnership.co.uk

Nathanael Dorent

233 Rue Marcadet

75018 Paris

+33 (0) 9 80 88 20 15

contact@nathanaeldorent.com

www.nathanaeldorent.com

Elder and Cannon

40 Berkeley Street

Glasgow G3 7DW

+44 (0) 141 204 1833

mail@elder-cannon.co.uk

www.elder-cannon.co.uk

Fife Architects

21 Cunzie Street

Anstruther

Fife KY10 3DF

+44 (0) 1333 310 551

enquiries@fifearchitects.com

www.fifearchitects.com

154 156 158

56 60

168

172 174

Malcolm Fraser Architects

c/o 6 Hartington Place

Edinburgh EH10 4LE

HLM Architects

2nd Floor, Ailsa Court

121 West Regent Street

Glasgow G2 2SD

+44 (0) 141 226 8320

amy.barrett@hlmarchitects.com

www.hlmarchitects.com

Hurd Rolland

Rossend Castle

Burntisland KY3 0DF

+44 (0) 1592 873 535

rossend@hurdrolland.co.uk

www.hurdrolland.co.uk

ISA

4-5 Blenheim Place

Edinburgh EH7 5JH

+44 (0) 131 229 6444

mail@isarchitects.co.uk

www.isarchitects.co.uk

48 52 54

198

62

126

Richard Gibson Architects Ltd

72a Commercial Street

Lerwick

Shetland ZE1 0DL

+44 (0) 1595 695 000

mail@rg-architects.com

www.rg-architects.com

John C Hope Architects

3 St Bernard's Crescent

Edinburgh EH4 1NR

+44 (0) 131 315 2215

jchope@mac.com

Hyve Architects Ltd

43 Evan Street

Stonehaven AB39 2ET

+44 (0) 1569 763 579

nikki.ritchie@hyvearch.co.uk

www.hyvearch.co.uk

Lily Jencks Studio

17 Powis Mews

London

+44 (0) 20 3489 2253

www.lilyjencksstudio.com

264

162 164 266

66 170

198

HAUS Collective

30 Bell Street

Glasgow G1 1LG

+44 (0) 141 552 8558

studio@haus-collective.com

www.haus-collective.com

Hoskins Architects

Studio 401 South Block

60-64 Osborne St

Glasgow G1 5QH

+44 (0) 141 553 5800

mail@hoskinsarchitects.co.uk

www.hoskinsarchitects.com

Icosis Architects

28 Albert Street

Edinburgh EH7 5LG

+44 (0) 131 555 2442

mail@icosis.co.uk

www.icosis.co.uk

jmarchitects

64 Queen Street

Edinburgh EH2 4NA

+44 (0) 131 464 6100

edinburgh@jmarchitects.net

www.jmarchitects.net

176

kalm architecture llp

Ferrygate Steading

North Berwick EH39 5DJ

+44 (0) 1620 850 649

kalm@kalmarchitecture.co.uk

www.kalmarchitecture.co.uk

184   186

LBA

18 Walker Street

Edinburgh EH3 7LP

+44 (0) 131 226 7186

mail@studiolba.co.uk

www.studiolba.co.uk

268

Loader & Monteith Architects

The Printworks

10 Otago Street

Glasgow G12 8JH

+44 (0) 141 334 3301

matt@loadermonteith.co.uk

www.loadermonteith.co.uk

80   270

McInnes Gardner Architects

7 Lynedoch Crescent

Glasgow G3 6DZ

+44 (0) 141 332 3841

info@mcinnesgardner.co.uk

www.mcinnesgardner.com

178

John Kinsley Architects

26 Bath Street

Edinburgh EH15 1HD

+44 (0) 7908 027054

john@johnkinsleyarchitects.co.uk

www.johnkinsleyarchitects.co.uk

188

LDN Architects

57-59 Bread Street

Edinburgh EH3 9AH

+44 (0) 131 222 2900

architects@ldn.co.uk

www.ldn.co.uk

76

Helen Lucas Architects

31-35 Marchmont Road

Edinburgh EH9 1HU

+44 (0) 131 478 8880

mail@helenlucas.co.uk

www.helenlucas.co.uk

82   84

Moxon Architects Ltd

Ardoch

Crathie

Ballater AB35 5UN

+44 (0) 1339 742 047

info@moxonarchitects.com

www.moxonarchitects.com

180   182

Konishi Gaffney Architects

88 Constitution Street

Edinburgh EH6 6RP

+44 (0) 131 555 4939

mail@konishigaffney.com

www.konishigaffney.com

70   72

LJR+H Chartered Architects

18 South Tay Street

Dundee DD1 1PD

+44 (0) 1382 200 511

admin@ljrh.co.uk

www.ljrh.co.uk

78

MAC Architects Ltd

24 Old Meldrum Road

Newmachar

Aberdeen AB21 0PJ

+44 (0) 1651 862 688

info@mac-architects.co.uk

www.mac-architects.co.uk

190   194   196

Richard Murphy Architects

The Breakfast Mission

15 Old Fishmarket Close

Edinburgh EH1 1RW

+44 (0) 131 220 6125

mail@richardmurphyarchitects.com

www.richardmurphyarchitects.com

274

Ann Nisbet Studio

4/2 996 Pollokshaws Rd

Glasgow G41 2HA

+44 (0) 7786 083 937

studio@annnisbet.com

www.annnisbet.com

206

Ian Parsons Architect

Gareview

Barr's Brae Lane

Port Glasgow PA14 5QA

+44 (0) 1475 742 848

info@ianparsonsarchitect.co.uk

www.ianparsonsarchitect.co.uk

278

Riach Partnership Ltd

200 Bath Street

Glasgow G2 4HG

+44 (0) 141 353 1230

mail@riach.co.uk

www.riach.co.uk

102

SBA Architects Ltd

Marybank Lodge

Marybank

Stornoway Castle Grounds

Stornoway HS2 0DD

+44 (0) 1851 704 889

sbaarchitects@btconnect.com

www.sbaarchitects.org

198   202   204

Oberlanders Architects LLP

16 Melville Street

Edinburgh EH3 7NS

+44 (0) 131 225 9070

mail@oberlanders.co.uk

www.oberlanders.co.uk

90

Fergus Purdie Architects

5A Melville Street

Perth PH1 5PY

+44 (0) 1738 444 122

fergus@ferguspurdiearchitect.co.uk

www.ferguspurdiearchitect.co.uk

94   96   98

Rural Design Architects

The Green

Portree

Isle of Skye IV51 9BT

+44 (0) 1478 613 379

studio@ruraldesign.net

www.ruraldesign.co.uk

106

Kerry Smith Architects

Studio Four

4 John Street

Montrose DD10 8LY

+44 (0) 1674 660 516

info@kerrysmitharchitects.co.uk

www.kerrysmitharchitects.co.uk

86

Paper Igloo Ltd

Ostro

Fintry Road

Kippen FK8 3HL

+44 (0) 1786 870 539

mhairi@paperigloo.com

www.paperigloo.com

92

Raw Architecture Workshop

Basement

2-5 St John's Square

Clerkenwell

London EC1M 4DE

info@rawarchitectureworkshop.com

www.rawarchitectureworkshop.com

126

Savills (UK) Ltd

28 Castle Street

Dumfries DG1 1DG

+44 (0) 1387 274 669

mleybourne@savills.com

www.savills.co.uk

208   210

Smith Scott Mullan Associates

378 Leith Walk

Edinburgh EH7 4PF

+44 (0) 131 555 1414

mail@smith-scott-mullan.co.uk

www.smith-scott-mullan.co.uk

212

108   110

112   222

224

Somner Macdonald Architects

126/2 Calton Road

Edinburgh EH8 8JQ

+44 (0) 131 558 7575

studio@somnermacdonald.co.uk

www.somnermacdonald.co.uk

studioKAP architects

Studio 9B

93-97 St George's Road

Glasgow G3 6JA

+44 (0) 141 552 2265

mail@studiokap.com

www.studiokap.com

WT Architecture Ltd

4-6 Gote Lane

South Queensferry

Edinburgh EH30 9PS

+44 (0) 131 331 2813

mail@wtarchitecture.com

www.wtarchitecture.com

ZONE Architects

211 Granton Road

Edinburgh EH5 1HD

+44 (0) 131 551 1973

info@zonearchitects.co.uk

www.zonearchitects.co.uk

216

218

130   134

Studio DuB

17A/2 West Crosscauseway

Edinburgh EH8 9JW

+44 (0) 131 668 1536

studiodub@mac.com

www.studiodub.co.uk

Sutherland Hussey Harris

99 Giles Street

Edinburgh EH6 6BZ

+44 (0) 131 553 4321

architecture@sutherlandhussey.co.uk

www.sutherlandhussey.co.uk

Simon Winstanley Architects

190 King Street

Castle Douglas DG7 1DB

+44 (0) 1556 503 826

email@simonwinstanley.com

www.simonwinstanley.com

Acknowledgements

WE ARE GRATEFUL TO THE following for their contributions to our first 2020 Visions publication:

Idea and Editor: Neil Baxter Hon FRIAS Hon FRIAS
Design: Jon Jardine (a special thanks to Jon for re-drawing all of the plans)
Produced by: The Royal Incorporation of Architects in Scotland as part of the Festival of Architecture 2017

With special thanks to Fiona Hyslop MSP, Cabinet Secretary for Culture, Tourism and External Affairs for the foreword and RIAS President, Stewart Henderson PRIAS for his introduction.

Many thanks also to the judges who selected our "top 100" from 237 submissions: the, London based, French architect Cecile Brisac RIBA; RIAS Lifetime Achievement Award winning architect, Tom Elder FRIAS; our President, Stewart Henderson PRIAS; the long-term social housing client, Rob Joiner Hon FRIAS, formerly of Reidvale and Molendinar Park Housing Associations; Christine Palmer FRIAS, also an architect and until recently, President of the Dundee Institute of Architects and the book's editor, RIAS Secretary and Treasurer, Neil Baxter Hon FRIAS Hon FRIBA.

Very special thanks, of course, to all the practices who subscribed to this publication and have contributed their superb projects, words, plans and images and to the photographers, some of Scotland's finest, whose work helps all 100 projects to shine.

The Royal Incorporation of Architects in Scotland
15 Rutland Square
Edinburgh EH1 2BE
+44 (0) 131 229 7545
info@rias.org.uk www.rias.org.uk